CENSUS OF INDIA 1911

Census of India 1871-1951, 9 Sets In 384 Bindings (9788121258876) Rs. 700000

Census of India 1911, 23 Vols. In 41 Bindings (9788121271271) Rs. 69000

1. India - Report (9788121275071) Rs. 2475 (Vol. I, Pt. 1)
2. India - Tables (9788121275057) Rs. 2225 (Vol. I, Pt. 2)
3. Andaman and Nicobar Islands - Report & Tables (9788121275033) Rs. 900 (Vol. II, Pt. 1 & 2)
4. Assam - Report (9788121275019) Rs. 1000 (Vol. III, Pt. 1)
5. Assam - Tables (9788121274999) Rs. 1300 (Vol. III, Pt. 2)
6. Baluchistan - Report & Tables (9788121274975) Rs. 950 (Vol. IV, Pt. 1 & 2)
7. Bengal, Bihar And Orissa And Sikkim - Report (9788121274951) Rs. 3100 (Vol. V, Pt. 1)
8. Bengal - Tables (9788121274937) Rs. 2250 (Vol. V, Pt. 2)
9. Bihar And Orissa - Tables and Bengal And Sikkim - Chapter I of Administrative Volume (9788121274913) Rs. 1800 (Vol. V, Pt. 3 & 4)
10. City of Calcutta - Report and Tables and Administrative (9788121274876) Rs. 1300 (Vol. VI, Pt. 1 & 2 & 3)
11. Bombay - Report (9788121274814) Rs. 1950 (Vol. VII, Pt. 1)
12. Bombay - Imperial Tables and Administrative Report (9788121274791) Rs. 3300 (Vol. VII, Pt. 2 & 3)
13. Bombay (Town And Island) - Report And Tables (9788121274753) Rs. 1250 (Vol. VIII, Pt. 1 & 2)
14. Burma - Report (9788121274739) Rs. 2250 (Vol. IX, Pt. 1)
15. Burma - Tables (9788121274715) Rs. 1480 (Vol. IX, Pt. 2)
16. Central Provinces And Berar - Report (9788121274692) Rs. 1475 (Vol. X, Pt. 1)
17. Central Provinces And Berar - Tables (9788121274678) Rs. 1900 (Vol. X, Pt. 2)
18. Coorg - Report And Tables Madras - Report (9788121274630) Rs. 1740 (Vol. XI & Vol. XII, Pt. 1)
19. Madras - Imperial And Provincial Tables (9788121274616) Rs. 1500 (Vol. XII, Pt. 2)
20. Madras - Administrative Report and city of Madras (9788121274593) Rs. 630 (Vol. XII, Pt. 3 & 4)
21. North - West Frontier Province - Report & Tables (9788121274579) Rs. 2150 (Vol. XIII, Pt. 1 & 2)
22. Punjab - Report (9788121274555) Rs. 3000 (Vol. XIV, Pt. 1)
23. Punjab - Tables (9788121274531) Rs. 2200 (Vol. XIV, Pt. 2)
24. Punjab - Appendices To The - Imperial Tables (9788121274517) Rs. 950 (Vol. XIV, Pt. 3)
25. United Provinces of Agra And Oudh - Report (9788121274494) Rs. 2225 (Vol. XV, Pt. 1)
26. United Provinces of Agra And Oudh - Tables (9788121274470) Rs. 4000 (Vol. XV, Pt. 2)
27. United Provinces of Agra And Oudh - Provincial Tables And Appendices (9788121274456) Rs. 570 (Vol. XV, Pt. 3)
28. Baroda - Report (9788121274432) Rs. 2000 (Vol. XVI, Pt. 1)
29. Baroda State - The Imperial Tables (9788121274418) Rs. 850 (Vol. XVI, Pt. 2)
30. Central India Agency - Report And Tables (9788121274395) Rs. 1470 (Vol. XVII)
31. Cochin - Report And Imperial Tables (9788121274371) Rs. 1150 (Vol. XVIII, Pt. 1 & 2)
32. Hyderabad State - Report (9788121274357) Rs. 890 (Vol. XIX, Pt. 1)
33. Hyderabad State - Imperial And Provincial Tables (9788121274333) Rs. 1750 (Vol. XIX, Pt. 2)
34. Kashmir - Report (9788121274319) Rs. 950 (Vol. XX, Pt. 1)
35. Kashmir - Tables (9788121274296) Rs. 1170 (Vol. XX, Pt. 2)
36. Mysore - Report (9788121274272) Rs. 1200 (Vol. XXI, Pt. 1)
37. Mysore - Tables (9788121274258) Rs. 1500 (Vol. XXI, Pt. 2)
38. Rajputana And Ajmer-Merwara - Report (9788121274234) Rs. 1470 (Vol. XXII, Pt. 1)
39. Rajputana And Ajmer-Merwara - Tables (9788121274210) Rs. 1700 (Vol. XXII, Pt. 2)
40. Travancore - Report (9788121274197) Rs. 1870 (Vol. XXIII, Pt. 1)
41. Travancore - Imperial Tables (9788121274173) Rs. 870 (Vol. XXIII, Pt. 2)

Owing to the antiquity and rarity of this book, certain pages are regrettably absent, and readability is compromised due to the blurring of the original text. If you possess any insights regarding the availability of these missing sections, kindly inform us. Your assistance is crucial in ensuring the completion of this significant work for the benefit of future generations.

CENSUS OF INDIA, 1911

VOLUME - VI

CITY OF CALCUTTA

PART I - REPORT

PART II - TABLES

PART III - ADMINISTRATIVE VOLUME

L. S. S. O'MALLEY

GYAN

Published by

Gyan Publishing House
5, Ansari Road
Daryaganj, New Delhi-110002
Phone: 011-47034999, 9811692060
E-mail: books@gyanbooks.com

Distribution Network
gyanbooks.com
India, USA, Canada, UK, Australia

ISBN: 978-81-212-7127-1 (Set) 23 Vols. In 41 Bindings

ISBN: 978-81-212-7487-6 (PB) Vol. VI, Pt. I, II, III

First Published, 1913

2nd Impression 2024

Printed at: Gyan Press, Delhi.

CENSUS OF INDIA 1911

CENSUS OF INDIA, 1911.

VOLUME VI.

CITY OF CALCUTTA.

PART I.

REPORT

BY

L. S. S. O'MALLEY,
OF THE INDIAN CIVIL SERVICE,
FELLOW OF THE ROYAL STATISTICAL SOCIETY,
SUPERINTENDENT OF CENSUS OPERATIONS, BENGAL.

CALCUTTA:
BENGAL SECRETARIAT BOOK DEPÔT.
1913.

Published at the BENGAL SECRETARIAT BOOK DEPÔT,
Writers' Buildings, Calcutta.

OFFICIAL AGENTS.

In India—

MESSRS. THACKER, SPINK & Co., Calcutta and Simla.
MESSRS. NEWMAN & Co., Calcutta.
MESSRS. HIGGINBOTHAM & Co., Madras.
MESSRS. THACKER & Co., LD., Bombay.
MESSRS. A. J. COMBRIDGE & Co., Bombay.
THE SUPERINTENDENT, AMERICAN BAPTIST MISSION PRESS, Rangoon.
MRS. RADHABAI ATMARAM SAGOON, Bombay.
MESSRS. R. CAMBRAY & Co., Calcutta.
RAI SAHIB M. GULAB SINGH & SONS, Proprietors of the Mufid-i-am Press, Lahore, Punjab.
MESSRS. THOMPSON & Co., Madras.
MESSRS. S. MURTHY & Co., Madras.
MESSRS. GOPAL NARAYAN & Co., Bombay.
MESSRS. B. BANERJEE & Co., 25, Cornwallis Street, Calcutta.
MESSRS. S. K. LAHIRI & Co., Printers and Booksellers, College Street, Calcutta.
MESSRS. V. KALYANARAMA IYER & Co., Booksellers, etc., Madras.
MESSRS. D. B. TARAPOREVALA, SONS & Co., Booksellers, Bombay.
MESSRS. G. A. NATESAN & Co., Madras.
MR. N. B. MATHUR, Superintendent, Nazir Kanun Hind Press, Allahabad.
THE CALCUTTA SCHOOL BOOK SOCIETY.
MR. SUNDER PANDURANG, Bombay.
MESSRS. A. M. & J. FERGUSON, Ceylon.
MESSRS. TEMPLE & Co., Madras.
MESSRS. COMBRIDGE & Co., Madras.
MESSRS. A. CHAND & Co., Lahore.
BABU S. C. TALUKDAR, Proprietor, Students & Co., Cooch Behar.
MESSRS. RAMCHANDRA GOVIND AND SON, Booksellers and Publishers, Kalbadevi, Bombay.
MESSRS. BUTTERWORTH & Co. (INDIA), LD., Calcutta.
THE WELDON LIBRARY, 18-5, Chowringhee Road, Calcutta.

In Great Britain—

MESSRS. A. CONSTABLE & Co., 10, Orange Street, Leicester Square, London, W. C.
MESSRS. GRINDLAY & Co., 54, Parliament Street, London, S. W.
MESSRS. KEGAN, PAUL, TRENCH, TRÜBNER & Co., 68-74, Carter Lane, London, E. C.
MR. B. QUARITCH, 11, Grafton Street, New Bond Street, London, W.
MESSRS. W. THACKER & Co., 2, Creed Lane, Ludgate Hill, London, E. C.
MESSRS. P. S. KING & SON, 2 & 4, Great Smith Street, Westminster, London, S. W.
MESSRS. H. S. KING & Co., 65, Cornhill, London, E. C.
MR. B. H. BLACKWELL, 50-51, Broad Street, Oxford.
MESSRS. DEIGHTON BELL & Co., Trinity Street, Cambridge.
MR. T. FISHER UNWIN, 1, Adelphi Terrace, London, W. C.
MESSRS. LUZAC & Co., 46, Great Russell Street, London, W. C.
MESSRS. OLIVER & BOYD, Tweeddale Court, Edinburgh.
MESSRS. E. PONSONBY, Limited, 116, Grafton Street, Dublin.

On the Continent—

MESSRS. R. FRIEDLÄNDER & SOHN, 11, Carlstrasse, Berlin, N. W., 6.
MR. OTTO HARRASSOWITZ, Leipzig, Germany.
MR. KARL W. HIERSEMANN, 29, Königsstrasse, Leipzig, Germany.
MR. ERNEST LEROUX, Rue Bonaparté, Paris, France.
MR. MARTINUS NIJHOFF, The Hague, Holland.

TABLE OF CONTENTS.

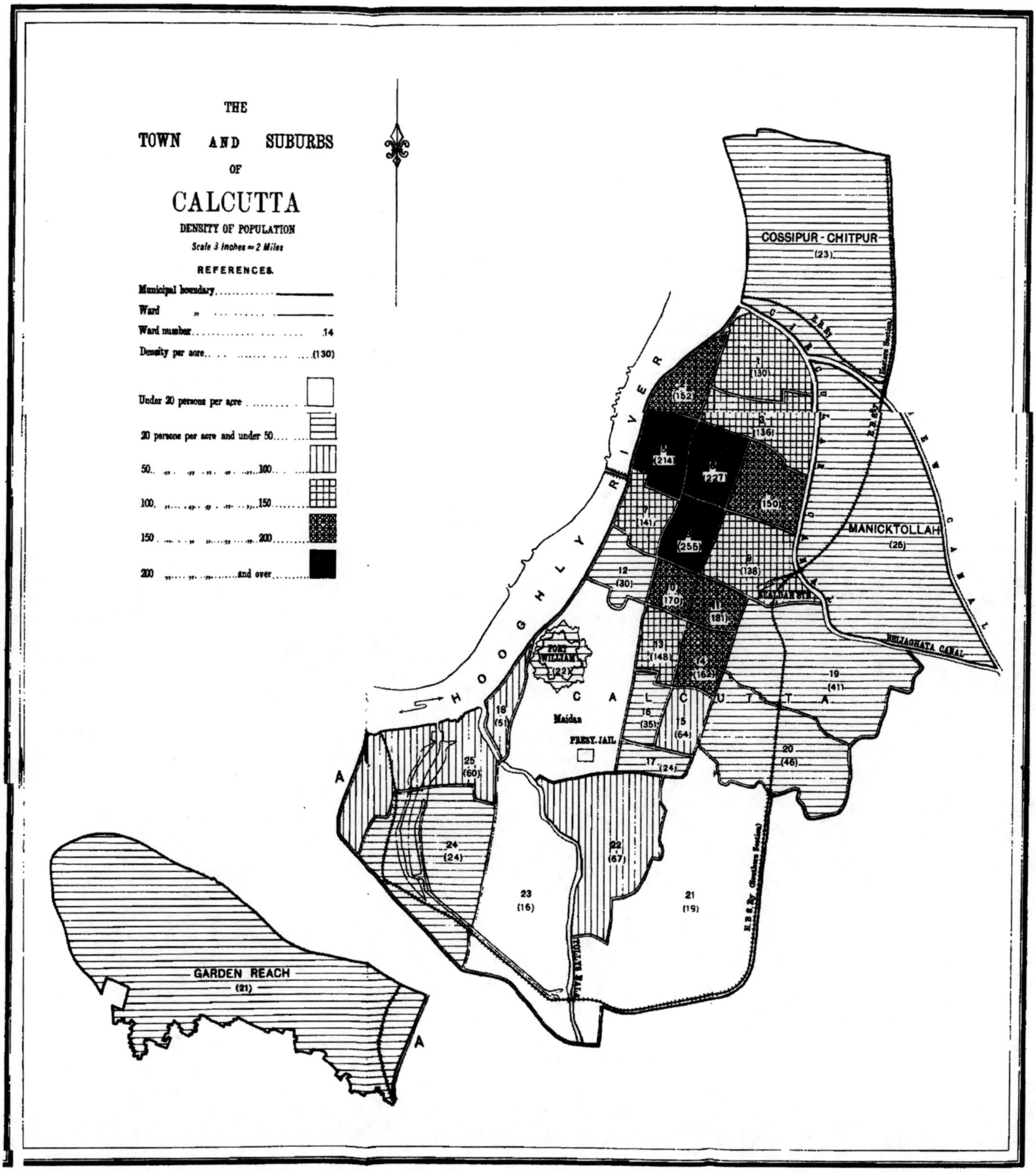
THE
TOWN AND SUBURBS
OF
CALCUTTA
DENSITY OF POPULATION
Scale 3 Inches = 2 Miles
REFERENCES.
Municipal boundary
Ward „
Ward number 14
Density per acre (130)
Under 20 persons per acre
20 persons per acre and under 50
50 „ „ „ „ „ 100
100 „ „ „ „ „ 150
150 „ „ „ „ „ 200
200 „ „ „ and over
COSSIPUR-CHITPUR
(23)
MANICKTOLLAH
(25)
HOOGHLY RIVER
CALCUTTA
FORT WILLIAM
(22)
Maidan
PRESY. JAIL
SEALDAH STN.
BELIAGHATA CANAL
GARDEN REACH
(21)
A
A

REPORT

ON THE CENSUS OF THE

CITY OF CALCUTTA, 1911.

CHAPTER I.

VARIATIONS IN THE POPULATION.

INTRODUCTORY.

THIS Report deals with the census of the city of Calcutta and the three suburban municipalities of Cossipur-Chitpur, Manicktollah and Garden Reach. The city of Calcutta includes not only the municipal area under the administration of the Corporation, but also the Port and Canals, Fort William and the Maidan. The suburban municipalities, which, for the sake of brevity, are referred to as the Suburbs, form part of the district of the 24-Parganas and are under a different system of municipal government. Their administration is regulated by the Bengal Municipal Act, and each has a separate constitution, which is distinct from that of Calcutta. They are, however, connected with Calcutta by a continuous line of buildings, and are structurally an integral part of it. With the exception, moreover, of part of Garden Reach, the Suburbs are under the control of the Commissioner of Police in Calcutta. For all practical purposes they may be regarded as forming part of the same city.

AREA AND POPULATION.

2. The aggregate area of Calcutta and the Suburbs is 42 square miles, of which Calcutta accounts for 32 square miles. The area within the jurisdiction of the Corporation is 18⅔ square miles, while the Port extends over 11 square miles, the remainder being made up by Fort William and the Maidan (2 square miles) and by the Canals (270 acres). The Suburbs have altogether an area of 10 square miles, which is evenly distributed among the three municipalities. The census of 1911 shows that the total population is 1,043,307, which is more than thrice that of Delhi, while it exceeds by 62,862 that of Bombay, the second most populous city in India. With the exception of London, no other city in the British Empire has so many inhabitants, and it takes its place among the twelve largest cities in the world.

PREVIOUS ESTIMATES AND ENUMERATIONS.

3. In the early days of British rule estimates of the population of Calcutta were made from time to time, but owing to their uncertain basis and the extension of the limits of the town, these estimates are of little practical value. The population in 1710 was only 10,000 or 12,000, but the settlement grew rapidly and by the middle of the eighteenth century the number of inhabitants is estimated to have exceeded 100,000 in the area owned by the Company, or double that figure, if the area owned by private zamindars is taken into account The subsequent estimates vary greatly. In 1831 Captain Birch, the Superintendent of Police, made a rough census extending over eight months, and returned the aggregate at 229,305, of whom 144,493 were males and 84,812 were females. The preponderance of males is interesting as showing that the disproportion of the sexes which is so noticeable a feature of the modern population is no new thing. The daily influx of workers from outside was also characteristic of Calcutta in the first year of Queen Victoria's reign, an enumeration held by Captain Birch showing that 177,000 persons entered the town between 4 A.M. and 11 P.M.* In 1840 it was estimated that the number of residents was 357,660 (on the basis of 5

* Bengal and Agra Gazetteer, 1841.

persons to every house or hut), and it seems probable that by 1850 it was at least 400,000.

4. The first census was held in 1872, when a population of 633,009 was returned for the area now included in Calcutta. Four years later a second enumeration was carried out in consequence of a general belief in the inaccuracy of the first census, but its result was to show a decline of 21,225, while in 1881 there was an addition of 523 only. At each subsequent census, however, there has been a substantial increase, as shown in the marginal statement. Calcutta is more populous by 42 per cent. than it was in 1872, but the growth of population has been relatively more rapid in the Suburbs, where there has been an addition of 66 per cent.

Census.	Calcutta.			Suburbs.		
	Population.	Actual increase.	Increase per cent.	Population.	Actual increase.	Increase per cent.
1891 ...	682,305	69,998	11·4	87,508	633	0·7
1901 ...	847,796	165,491	24·3	101,348	13,840	15·8
1911 ...	896,067	48,271	5·7	147,240	45,893	45·3

5. Before proceeding to discuss the results of the last census, reference may be made to some of the conditions affecting the growth of population in Calcutta. In the first place, the population is peculiarly constituted, there being a large excess of males, a comparatively small number of women of child-bearing age, and a relative paucity of children. A large proportion of the inhabitants are immigrants attracted by the prospects of obtaining employment at good wages in the metropolis. Among them males predominate, for most are temporary immigrants, who leave their wives behind and look forward to returning home when they have accumulated sufficient funds. There are roughly two males to every female, and the tendency is for the disparity of the sexes to grow greater. The number of women of child-bearing age, *i.e.*, women aged 15 to 40, is unusually small, their proportion to the total population being only 15 per cent., whereas the ratio in Bengal is 21 per cent. Further evidence of the narrow limits within which an increase by reproduction can be expected is afforded by the returns for married females of child-bearing age, who represent only 10 per cent. of the population, or 5 per cent. less than in Bengal. If prostitutes of this age who returned themselves as married are excluded, the proportion falls to a little under 10 per cent. The birth-rate in these circumstances cannot but be small, and another factor which operates as a check is the use of preventive means.

CONDITIONS AFFECTING GROWTH.

6. Apart from these factors, the number of births in Calcutta is reduced by the custom of women leaving the city for their confinements: it is estimated that nearly one-fifth of the births take place in their native villages. These births, consequently, do not find an entry in the returns for Calcutta. On the other hand, as the mothers return shortly afterwards with their infants, the deaths among the latter help to swell the infant death-roll of Calcutta, which is extraordinarily high. The average number of deaths among children under 1 year of age during the decade ending in 1910 was no less than 16 per cent. of the total deaths and 31 per cent. of the births: in other words, out of every three children brought into the world, one dies within a year. The causes of this high death-rate will be dealt with in Chapter II, and here it will be sufficient to state that it is the combined result of several causes, among which the most potent are premature birth and debility at birth, bad midwifery and *tetanus neonatorum* due to the umbilical cord being cut with dirty instruments. The combined effect of a low birth-rate and high infantile mortality is to make the number of children in Calcutta unusually small, those under 15 years of age representing less than one-fourth of the total population.

7. The average annual birth-rate of Calcutta for the decade ending in 1910 was only 17·7 per mille on the population of 1901. The death-rate, on the other hand, was 34·9 per mille, the net result being an excess of deaths over births amounting to 145,534. The mortality is surprisingly high, considering that children, among whom there is always a high death-rate, are comparatively few, while young adult males in the prime of life are unusually numerous; those between 20 and 50 years of age account for 43 per cent. of the total population. On the other hand, the improvements in drainage and sanitation effected during

VITAL STATISTICS.

the last 10 years appear to be making a rapid change in the chances of life of the inhabitants. The excess of deaths over births has declined steadily since 1901, and rapidly since 1907. From the statistics in Subsidiary Table III at the end of this Chapter it will be seen that the excess of deaths over births was reduced during the decade by nearly one-fourth.

8 The same subsidiary table shows the mortality due to different causes during the decade. These figures are much more reliable than those compiled in other towns and districts. As nearly every death is enquired into by a special officer, they may be taken as approximately correct. Plague has caused the greatest mortality, being responsible for nearly one-sixth of the deaths. Fever and pulmonary affections come next. Malaria is seldom contracted within the limits of the old town, and causes the greatest mortality in the suburban wards and added areas. The number of deaths due to lung diseases, which are far commoner in India than is usually supposed, is a testimony to the accuracy of diagnosis. Cholera, dysentery and diarrhœa, taken together are responsible for a death-roll exceeding even that of plague. Small-pox is a minor cause of death; the small mortality due to it, in spite of epidemics in four years, is an object lesson to less advanced municipalities. Cholera is most prevalent in the area situated near the Canal and Tolly's Nullah, and the mortality among Hindus is relatively greater than among Musalmans. These two facts are connected with the same cause, viz., that the Hindus frequently bathe in Tolly's Nullah and drink its sacred, but polluted, water instead of the filtered water supply. Hindus also suffer from small-pox more than the followers of other religions, from which it would appear that their children are less protected by vaccination. The incidence of diarrhœa and dysentery is greatest in the suburban wards, probably because service privies of a bad design are commoner in the outskirts of the town than in wards where the water-carriage system is in vogue.

VARIATIONS SINCE 1901.

9. In Calcutta the census discloses a net addition of 48,27ı or 5·7 per cent., which is entirely due to the influx of immigrants, *i.e.*, persons born outside Calcutta, who are now more numerous by 82,209 than in 1901: males alone contribute 69,523 to this number. There has, however been a loss on account of the exodus of those born in Calcutta, the emigrant population having increased by 51,828, so that the actual balance of migration in favour of Calcutta, compared with 1901, is only 30,38ı. As will be shewn later, however, it is more than probable that a large number of those enumerated in Garden Reach, who returned their birth place as Calcutta, were really born in Garden Reach and should not therefore be classed among the emigrants from Calcutta. If this hypothesis if accepted, the emigrant population is smaller and the real gain from migration is greater than the figures would indicate.

CALCUTTA.	1911. Male.	1911. Female.	1901. Male.	1901. Female.
Actual population ...	607,674	288,493	562,596	285,200
Immigrants	471,125	168,223	401,002	155,537
Emigrants	47,544	40,204	17,922	18,898
Natural population ..	184,493	160,874	178,916	148,061

10. The Suburbs have developed far more rapidly than Calcutta, having an aggregate increment of 45,892 persons, or 45·3 per cent. The most progressive of the municipalities is Manicktollah, which has added 66 per cent. to its numbers. It is closely followed by Garden Reach with 60·6 per cent., while Cossipur-Chitpur is content with a more modest advance of 18·2 per cent. The increase in Manicktollah and Cossipur-Chitpur is nearly entirely due to the greater influx of immigrants,* the extent of which may be gauged by the marginal figures. In Garden Reach the addition of 17,084 persons is partly the result of an extension of the municipal boundary, the added area having a population of 6,444 or one-third of the net gain. It is also partly due to industrial development: at the time of the census no less than 10,460 males, or nearly two-fifths of the total male population, were employed in its jute mills, cotton mills and

MUNICIPALITY.	Increase since 1901. Total.	Increase since 1901. Immigrant.
Cossipur-Chitpur	7,428	5,916
Manicktollah	21,380	19,296
Garden Reach	17,084	28,557
Total Suburbs ...	45,892	53,709

* Immigrants in this case means persons born outside the district of the 24-Parganas and includes persons born in Calcutta.

dockyards. Altogether 21,986 persons, or nearly half the town population, returned their birthplace as Calcutta, and only 2,797 were recorded as born in the 24-Parganas, whereas the corresponding figures in 1901 were 1,865, and 14,270, respectively. The figures are in themselves, so extraordinary that it seems certain that at this census persons born in Garden Reach returned themselves as born in Calcutta, not realizing that for administrative purposes Garden Reach forms part of the 24-Parganas and not of Calcutta.

11. That Calcutta should have increased by only 5·7 per cent. since 1901 seems *primâ facie* surprising, when it is remembered that between 1891 and 1901 it grew at the rate of 24 per cent., and that at this census the Suburbs have an increase of 45·3 per cent. while Howrah has added 13·6 per cent. to the number of its inhabitants. The expansion in the preceding decade was, however, not altogether so great as would appear from the figures, for the census of 1901 was more complete than that of 1891, and the true rate of increase was less than that actually returned. Since 1901, moreover, great changes have taken place in Calcutta, especially in connection with the fringe area and suburban drainage schemes. The systematic improvement of the insanitary blocks of huts known as *bastis* has also been taken in hand. In cases where the landlords were unwilling to carry out the sanitary improvements prescribed, *bastis* have had to be removed entirely, the land on which they stood being either left vacant or used for the construction of masonry buildings. In other cases, the *bastis* have been retained, but the lanes which traverse them have been widened, or new roads opened out, with a consequent reduction of congestion. During the six years of its existence the Basti Department has opened out 8 miles of roads and constructed 6 miles of sewers. These reforms have materially affected the distribution of the population, for the coolies who lived in the demolished huts have had to move out and find lodging elsewhere.

12. Further, the means of communication between Calcutta and its environs have been multiplied and improved, so that it is an easy matter for many thousands who work daily in Calcutta to live outside it. The Calcutta tramway system has been extended to Alipore, Tollygunge and Behala, as well as to Howrah. The ferry steamer services along and across the Hooghly have been increased and accelerated, while the suburban railway traffic has been developed. Between 1901 and 1910 the number of season tickets issued by the East Indian Railway to and from Howrah rose from 31,543 to 54,187 (an increase of 60 per cent.), and the aggregate of monthly ticket-holders on the Howrah-Amta and Howrah-Sheakhala Light Railways from 1,038 to 7,522. Decennial figures for the Bengal-Nagpur Railway are not available, but during the five years 1905-1910 the season tickets issued to and from Howrah increased from 6,118 to 9,792. On the Eastern Bengal State Railway, also, the facilities of suburban traffic are being more and more utilized, and in 1910 the number of season tickets issued to and from Sealdah was 31,766; of these 28,399 tickets were issued to Calcutta and only 2,367 from Calcutta. Figures for previous years are not available.

The result of these changes is a centrifugal tendency. Even those born in Calcutta are beginning to prefer to live in places outside it, from which they can travel in daily. At the time of the census half of the persons born in Calcutta who were enumerated outside it were found to be present in adjoining towns, viz., in round figures, 10,000 in Howrah, the same number in Manicktollah, 2,000 in Cossipur-Chitpur and 2,000 in Garden Reach.* Had the city-born population enumerated in Calcutta been the same as in 1901, the rate of growth would have been 9·8 per cent.

LOCAL VARIATIONS.†

13. For the discussion of the variations in different parts of Calcutta, it will be convenient to group the wards in 3 classes, viz., 1) the northern wards, Nos. 1-6, all of which are more populous than in 1901; (2) the central wards, Nos. 7-18, where there is a general loss of population except in Ward No. 11 (Paddapukur); and (3) the south and south-eastern wards, Nos. 19-25, which have all advanced.

* See, however, the preceding remarks about the number enumerated in Garden Reach.

† I desire to acknowledge my obligations to Babu Makhan Lal Ganguli of the Assessor's Department in the Calcutta Corporation for assistance in preparing this account of local variations.

CENTRAL BLOCK.

14. The central block consists of Barabazar, Kalutola, Muchipara, Bowbazar, Paddapukur, Waterloo Street, Fenwick Bazar, Taltola, Collinga, Park Street, Baman Bustee (Victoria Terrace) and Hastings. Nowhere has there been such a heavy loss of population as in the three wards which constitute the main European quarter of Calcutta, viz., Baman Bustee, where the decrease amounts to 43 per cent., Collinga (32 per cent.) and Park Street (13 per cent.). The decrease in these three wards is due mainly to the operation of the Bustee Regulations, which have been effectual in either reducing the congestion of *bastis* or sweeping them away altogether. The rise in rents and the development of trade have further contributed to the diminution of population. Landlords have demolished small *kutcha* buildings, and in their place have erected large masonry houses, either for use as shops or as residential quarters: in some cases also they have converted dwelling-houses or parts of them into shops. The heavy decrease in Baman Bustee (Ward No. 17) is partly due to the fact that in 1901 the Presidency Jail, with a population of 1,459, was treated as forming part of this ward, though the jail lies outside its limits. If its population is deducted from the figures for 1901, the decrease is reduced to 870. For this decrease the removal of *bastis* is entirely responsible. Ten years ago there were five big *bastis* containing 325 huts, which have been replaced by *pucca* residential houses, with large compounds, each ordinarily occupied by only one European family.

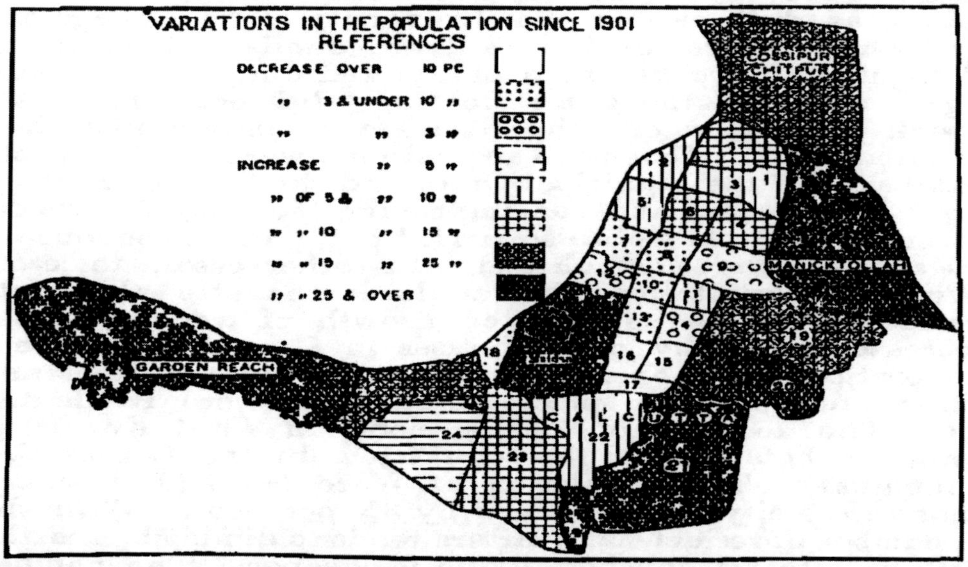

15. In Collinga (Ward No. 15) the structural changes have been more extensive, the number of *bastis* having been reduced from 99 to 54. All the larger *bastis* in the quarter inhabited by Europeans have been removed: those that are left are mainly small blocks in the Muhammadan quarters. A large plot of ground between Park Street on the north and Rawdon Street on the east, which abutted close upon Theatre Road on the south, was a few years ago studded with huts, but is now the site of about 15 European houses, each occupied by perhaps less than 20 persons including servants. Each *basti* contained on the average 23 occupied huts, so that if we assume that the number of persons in each hut was the same as the average (5) returned for occupied houses in this ward in 1901, the removal of the 45 *bastis* represents a displacement of 5,175 persons, a figure which closely corresponds with the loss (5,395) recorded at this census.

16. In Ward No. 16 (Park Street) four large *bastis*, containing over 150 huts or *kutcha* houses, have been removed, and residential houses intended for European tenants now occupy their sites: one of the *bastis* was large and populous enough to be valued at nearly Rs. 14,000 per annum for rateable purposes. The development of trade during the decade has also led to shops replacing houses. A number of new dwelling-houses have sprung up, it is true, but it is difficult to find any instance of a building having been constructed on a vacant site; the new houses have invariably been erected on old building sites.

17. The percentage of decrease in the other central wards varies greatly. It is less than ½ per cent. in Ward No. 12 (Waterloo Street) and Ward No. 14

(Taltola), and only 1 per cent. in ward No. 9 (Muchipara): these three wards may be described as stationary. In the remaining five wards (Hastings, Barabazar, Kalutola, Bowbazar and Fenwick Bazar) the loss varies from 3½ to nearly 10 per cent., the latter figure being reached in Ward No. 8 (Kalutola). In Kalutola the acquisition of land for the Presidency College and the Medical College Hospital, as well as for the University Law College and other public buildings, caused the removal of a large number of *bastis* and residential houses. Altogether 75 *bastis* were obliterated during the decade, but the corresponding increase in the *pucca* holdings did not exceed 47. In Ward No. 13 (Fenwick Bazar), where the decrease is only a little less, the same causes have been at work. Extensive acquisitions were made by the Corporation for the extension of the Municipal Office and the Sir Stuart Hogg Market, for opening out new roads, and for improving the neighbourhood. Eight large *basti*-improvement projects were also carried out, in consequence of which a number of *basti* huts were demolished. In other cases, to avoid the expense of improving their sanitation, the landlords converted them into vacant sites. Paradoxical as it may appear, the growth of trade has also contributed to the decrease, for many of the houses in Chowringhee Road, Corporation Street, Corporation Place, Free School Street, Lindsay Street and Wellesley Street, which are now shops or places of business, were residential premises ten years ago. The decrease of 7½ per cent. in Ward No. 10 is mainly due to *basti* improvements and to the acquisition by the Corporation of one large *basti* (Ghumghar). The population of Ward No. 7 (Barabazar), which is a centre of trade in the city, has declined by 3½ per cent. With the growth of its trade the number of residential quarters tends to diminish, and the excess population overflows into wards where living is cheaper. The number of *bastis* in this ward has also been reduced by 52 during the last 10 years, while the increase in *pucca* holdings is only 20. The loss in Ward No. 9 is dealt with below in the section dealing with the fringe area.

NORTHERN BLOCK.

18. In the northern block the rate of growth varies from 6 per cent. in Jorabagan to 14½ per cent. in Sukea Street. The comparatively low percentage of increase in Jorabagan (Ward No. 5) is attributable partly to the removal of *bastis* and partly to the fact that, this being a commercial quarter, the development of trade has led to residential houses or huts being transformed into shops and warehouses. In Ward No. 3 (Bartala) the increase of 9 per cent. is perhaps less than might have been expected in view of its having a comparatively low density and room for expansion, but here extensive acquisitions were made by the Corporation for the drainage of the fringe area.

SOUTHERN AND SOUTH-EASTERN BLOCK.

19. In the south of Calcutta the greatest expansion has taken place in Ward No. 21 (Ballygunge-Tollygunge), the addition being 12,745 or 47 per cent. Ten years ago this ward was the most thinly populated part of the city, there being only 13 persons per acre. Since that year the extension of the tramway service has attracted settlers, both European and Indian. A number of new residential houses have been constructed, the process being accelerated by the sale of municipal surplus lands on the Landsdowne Road and by the widening of the Hazra Road. The rapidity of growth (34 per cent.) in Ward No. 20 (Beniapukur) is little less remarkable: it is the result of the *basti* population from the neighbouring European wards (viz., Wards Nos. 15, 16 and 17) having overflowed into an area where there was room for expansion. As regards the other suburban wards, the increase of 17 per cent. in Ward No. 19 (Entally) is attributable to the movements of the people from the centre of the town to its outkirts. Its growth would have been much greater had not a number of *basti* huts and *pucca* buildings been removed on the south side of Beliaghatta Road and in Kamardanga, where land has been acquired by the Eastern Bengal State Railway and the Calcutta Corporation.

20. The increase of 11½ per cent. in Ward No. 23 (Alipore) is partly due to the transformation of the Penn estate into a European colony, and the erection of new buildings in the neighbourhood. The extension of the tramway through the ward has also attracted a considerable population to the Indian quarters, besides which some municipal surplus land on the Chetla Central Road was sold a few years ago and the plots

utilized for house-building. A larger increase might indeed have been expected, but the acquisitions made by the Port Commissioners have practically depopulated the extensive area lying between the Boat Canal and the Tollygunge Circular Road on one side and between Diamond Harbour Road and Tolly's Nullah on the other side. *Basti* lands have also been acquired by Government, the Port Commissioners and the Corporation, while considerable areas have been purchased and cleared by private parties. Ward No. 22 (Bhawanipore), which was in 1901 the most densely populated suburban ward, has added only 10 per cent. to its population, its advance having been checked by the necessities of sanitation. *Basti* improvements have been carried out and land acquired for the construction of roads and squares. Large *bastis* to the east of Lee Road have been gradually cleared of huts, which have been replaced by a number of residential houses, while the land on the other side of Chowringhee Road (between Lower Circular Road and Sambhu Nath Pandit Street) has been acquired by Government and cleared for a building site. Least progress has been made by Ward No. 24 (Ekbalpore), where the Port Commissioners have acquired considerable areas for the extension of Kidderpore Docks.

THE FRINGE AREA.

21. The fringe area consists of a strip of land to the east of Wards Nos. 1, 3, 4 and 9, which goes by the name of Ooltadanga in Ward No. 1, Manicktollah in Ward No. 3, and Beliaghatta in Wards Nos. 4 and 9. In all four wards the fringe area has added to its population, except in Ward No. 9, where there is a heavy loss, which is, however, partly compensated for by a gain in the remainder of the ward, as shown in the margin. In this portion of the fringe area there is not much room for expansion, as a large portion is occupied by the Sealdah railway station premises and the Calcutta Gas Works. A number of *bastis* have, moreover, been demolished during the course of the last ten years owing to the acquisitions made by the Corporation for the fringe area drainage project and by the railway for the extension of the station.

Ward.	Fringe area.		Remainder of ward.	
	1911.	1901.	1911.	1901.
1	9,662	8,506	43,374	38,381
3	13,692	13,472	40,918	36,744
4	13,739	11,676	34,373	30,358
9	6,966	11,709	56,396	52,407
Total ...	44,059	45,363	175,061	157,890

OTHER AREAS.

22. The variations in other areas call for few remarks, as their character is exceptional and no natural increase of population can be expected in them. Fort William and the Maidan, which are grouped together, contain 4,411* persons or 1,081 more than in 1901. The Port and Canals have, in more senses than one, a floating population, which varies with the number of steamers and boats present at the time of the census. In the Port 26,890 persons were enumerated on 3,445 vessels of various descriptions, such as steamers, boats, barges and flats: in the Canals the number was 3,265 and 595, respectively. The aggregate for the water area (30,155) represents 3·4 per cent. of the total population of Calcutta.

* The population of the Fort was 3,658 and of the Maidan 753. To the latter, however, should be added the population of the Presidency Jail (1,414), which for some unknown reason was treated as part of Ward No. 18 (Hastings).

SUBSIDIARY TABLE I—Variations in Population.

Wards.	Population in 1911.	Number of persons per acre.	Number of females to 1,000 males.	Percentage of Variation. 1901 to 1911.	1891 to 1901.	1881 to 1891.	1872 to 1881.	Net variation, 1872 to 1911.
CALCUTTA WITH SUBURBS	*1,043,307*	*39*	*495*	*+ 9·9*	*+23·3*	*+10·1*	*—3·1*	*+44·6*
CALCUTTA	*896,067*	*44*	*475*	*+ 5·7*	*+24·3*	*+11·4*	*—3·3*	*+41·6*
MUNICIPAL AREA	*861,601*	*72*	*502*	*+ 6·3*	*+ 24·7*	*+ 12·5*	*—6·6*	*+ 40·7*
Ward No. 1, Shampukur ...	53,036	130	685	+13·1	+ 27·1	+ 29·4	— 1·2	+ 83·8
" " 2, Kumartoli	33,073	152	565	+ 9·7	+ 13·3	+ 13·6	—24·5	— 2·8
" " 3, Bartala	54,610	136	666	+ 8·8	+ 37·8	+ 25·9	— 3·3	+ 82·5
" " 4, Sukea Street ...	48,112	150	623	+14·5	+ 20·7	+ 48·7	2·5	+ 99·2
" " 5, Jorabagan	52,114	214	441	+ 6·2	+ 25·2	+ 7·9	— 7·1	+ 33·4
" " 6, Jorasanko	59,541	227	579	+12·4	+ 27·2	+ 26·9	— 8 9	+ 65·3
" " 7, Barabazar	30,495	141	207	— 3·4	+ 52·0	— 0·6	—11·6	+ 29·7
" " 8, Kalutola	57,094	255	358	— 9·6	+ 24·4	+ 7·3	— 6·9	+ 12·4
" " 9, Muchipara ...	62,362	138	478	— 1·2	+ 29·6	+ 13·5	— 0 1	45·2
" " 10, Bowbazar	25,014	170	343	— 7·5	+ 19·3	+ 4·8	— 8·1	+ 6·2
" " 11, Paddapukur ...	29,968	181	571	+ 6·8	+ 35·2	+ 1·2	+ 0·1	+ 46·3
" " 12, Waterloo Street ..	6,284	30	111	— 0·3	+ 6·2	+ 2·5	+ 1·4	+ 10·2
" " 13, Fenwick Bazar ...	28,430	148	248	— 8·2	+ 10·0	+ 9·5	— 3·3	+ 6·2
" " 14, Taltola	32,112	162	472	— 0·4	+ 10·4	+ 12·1	— 3·0	+ 18·4
" " 15, Collinga	11,385	64	412	—32·2	+ 26·9	+ 11·6	— 7·3	— 10·9
" " 16, Park Street ...	5,294	35	182	—13·4	+ 32·3	— 7·0	+ 8·8	+ 15·9
" " 17, Baman Bustee (Victoria Terrace).	3,125	24	234	—42·7	+ 18·6	— 24·9	— 6·7	— 52·4
" " 18, Hastings	5,550	51	396	6·2	+ 22·8	— 5·8	— 0·7	+ 7·7
" " 19, Entally	45,072	41	587	+16·7	+ 14·0	+ 25·9	— 1·3	+ 65·3
" " 20, Beniapukur	37,881	46	634	+34·3	+ 22·5	+ 21·8	— 6·9	+ 86·7
" " 21, Ballygunge-Tollygunge.	39,952	19	683	+46·8	+ 19·2	+ 11·8	—12·5	+ 71·3
" " 22, Bhawanipore ...	54,569	67	653	+ 9·9	+ 16·6	+ 12·1	+ 2·4	+ 47·0
" " 23, Alipore	19,749	16	428	+11·5	+ 19·7	+ 10·2	—30·8	+ 1·7
" " 24, Ekbalpore	21,869	24	678	+ 1·2	+ 40·9	— 3·3	—12·2	21·0
" " 25, Watganj	43,806	60	391	+15·5	+ 41·3	— 3·9	21 2	+ 90·2
Fort William and Maidan	4,411	3	125	+32·5	— 8 0	+ 8·4	+34·5	+ 77·6
Port	26,890	4	4	— 9·7	+ 12·0	— 5·7	+69·3	+ 61·4
Canals	3,265	12	...	—26·6	+111·6	— 30·1	+70·8	+ 55·4
SUBURBS	*147,240*	*23*	*632*	*+45·3*	*+15·8*	*+ 0·7*	*— 2·0*	*+66·1*
Cossipur-Chitpur	48,178	23	555	+18·2	+ 29·7	+ 19·5	+ 3·6	+ 89·9
Manicktollah	53,767	25	694	+66·0	+ 15·0	— 41·5	—10·9	— 0·4
Garden Reach	45 295	21	637	+80·6	+ 1·0	+124·2	+34·5	+389·3

SUBSIDIARY TABLE II.—Comparison with Vital Statistics.

Locality.	In 1901-1910: Total number of— Births.	Deaths.	Number per cent. of Population of 1901 of— Births.	Deaths.	Excess (+) or deficiency (—) of Births over Deaths. Actual number.	Proportional figures.	Increase (+) or decrease (—) of population of 1911 compared with 1901. Natural population.	Actual population.
Calcutta with Suburbs ...	166,472	314,548	17·54	33·14	— 148,076	— 15·60	Not available	+ 94,163
Calcutta	150,199	295,733	17·72	34·88	— 145,534	— 17·16	+ 17,890	+ 48,271
Suburbs	16,273	18,815	16·06	18·56	— 2,542	— 2·50	Not available.	+ 45,892
Cossipur-Chitpur	5,000	5,869	12·27	14·40	— 869	— 2·13		+ 7,428
Manicktollah	5,170	6,314	15·96	19·50	— 1,144	— 3·54		+ 21,380
Garden Reach	6,103	6,632	21·63	23·51	— 529	— 1·88		+ 17,084

SUBSIDIARY TABLE III.—Vital Statistics of Calcutta.

Year.	Deaths from— Plague.	Fever.	Pulmonary affections.	Dysentery and diarrhoea.	Cholera.	Small-pox.	Other causes.	Total number of deaths.	Total number of births.	Excess of deaths over births.
1901	7,683	6,311	4,287	3,211	1,720	2,097	6,947	32,456	9,129	23,327
1902	7,278	5,593	3,129	3,206	2,716	127	9,361	31,410	12,122	19,288
1903	8,222	4,869	3,389	2,677	1,990	50	8,568	29,763	13,182	16,583
1904	4,689	4,907	3,773	2,509	2,056	74	9,315	27,323	15,250	12,073
1905	7,372	4,351	3,969	2,843	2,323	272	11,051	32,181	15,637	16,544
1906	2,606	3,886	4,384	2,734	2,504	2,905	11,274	30,293	15,083	15,210
1907	3,591	3,915	5,007	2,751	3,303	1,286	11,589	31,942	16,224	15,718
1908	1,779	2,997	5,156	2,312	3,694	578	11,173	27,689	17,043	10,646
1909	2,117	3,087	4,994	1,780	2,022	3,784	11,162	28,946	19,423	9,523
1910	1,262	3,043	4,781	1,807	1,901	48	10,886	23,728	17,106	6,622
TOTAL ...	*46,799*	*42,959*	*42,869*	*25,830*	*24,729*	*11,221*	*101,326*	*295,733*	*150,199*	*145,534*

Note—Deaths from pulmonary affections were not recorded separately in 1901, but grouped with deaths from other causes. The average annual mortality from these affections from 1902 to 1910 has therefore been taken as the figure for 1901.

CHAPTER II.

DISTRIBUTION OF POPULATION.

DENSITY.

23. THE average density of Calcutta and the Suburbs is 39 persons per acre, the figure for Calcutta being 44 and for the Suburbs 23 per acre. The average in Calcutta is, however, considerably reduced by the Port, Fort William and the Maidan, which extend over 13 square miles, or two-fifths of the total area of the city, but contribute less than a twenty-fifth of the total population. The marginal table shows the density per acre in the city, the municipal area and the Suburbs since 1881.

	1911.	1901.	1891.	1881.
Calcutta	44	41	33	30
Municipal area	72	68	54	48
Suburbs	23	16	14	13

CALCUTTA.

24. In the municipal area there are no less than 72 persons per acre, or 4 more than in 1901. With this teeming population the city proper is more densely populated than London (60 per acre). The local variations are very great, for three of the 25 wards contain over 200 persons per acre, 10 from 100 to 200, and 4 from 50 to 100, while in eight wards the ratio falls below 50 per acre. The maximum density (255) is found in Kalutola to the north, the minimum (16) in Alipore to the south. The largest ward, Ballygunge-Tollygunge, which extends over 2,067 acres, is one of the least populous, containing only 19 persons per acre. Bowbazar in the heart of town has one-fourteenth of its area, but is nine times as populous.

25. The eight most densely populated wards are shown in the margin. The first three form a solid block in the north of the old town, and they are surrounded by wards in which the density varies from 100 to 200. North of the Maidan there is only one ward, viz., No. 12 (Waterloo Street) in which there are less than 100 persons per acre. The latter, with 30 persons per acre, is one of the most thinly populated parts of the city, the explanation being that it is mainly occupied by large European shops, public buildings and offices, in addition to Government House. Land in this ward is too valuable to be utilized, to any considerable extent, for residential purposes, and the tramway system has rendered it possible for those engaged in business to reside elsewhere. All the wards in which there is a considerable European element, viz., Wards Nos. 15 to 18, 21 and 23, are thinly populated, as might be expected from the character of their houses, the mean varying from 16 to 64 per acre. All the suburban wards also are still comparatively thinly peopled, the greatest density being found in Bhawanipore, where it is 67 per acre.

Ward No.	Name.		Density per acre.
8	Kalutola	...	255
6	Jorasanko	...	227
5	Jorabagan	...	214
11	Paddapukur	...	181
10	Bowbazar	...	170
14	Taltola	...	162
2	Kumartoli	...	152
4	Sukea Street	...	150

SUBURBS.

26. The distribution of the population in the Suburbs is very uniform, the density per acre being 25 in Manicktollah, 23 in Cossipur-Chitpur and 21 in Garden Reach. There is, however, considerable disparity between the different wards as shown in the margin. In Cossipur-Chitpur, the most populous wards (Nos. 1 and 2) lie along the Hooghly. In Manicktollah density gradually increases from north to south. In Garden Reach it is highest in the circle next Calcutta, and gradually falls, the further one proceeds away from that city, the minimum being reached in the circle furthest removed from Calcutta.

Municipality.	WARD OR CIRCLE.			
	1	2	3	4
Cossipur-Chitpur	39	29	12	23
Manicktollah	20	24	26	...
Garden Reach	22	19	13	10

VARIATIONS IN DENSITY.

27. In the last Census Report of Calcutta it was stated:—"The remarkable increase in the case of the densely populated wards is chiefly to be explained by the fact that the natural tendency, in large cities, to an increase of congestion in areas already congested, unless checked by municipal action, is specially marked in Calcutta, where up-country immigrant labourers, who have recently come to the city, prefer to live with their friends in quarters already congested rather than to seek for more sanitary surroundings elsewhere." Since 1901 the action of the Corporation has been largely instrumental in preventing further undesirable increases in congested areas. Owing to the changes effected by the total or partial demolition of *bastis* by the Corporation, of which many instances have been given in the last Chapter, it is difficult to draw any definite conclusions regarding the extent to which density has affected the growth of population. In the second place, the consideration of the question of the correlation of density and variation is complicated by the fact that some congested wards are trade centres, where land is rising in value: consequently, the tendency is for shops, warehouses and other non-residential premises to replace dwelling-houses and huts. *Migration from such areas is due not to congestion, but to the interests of trade limiting the area available for accommodation.*

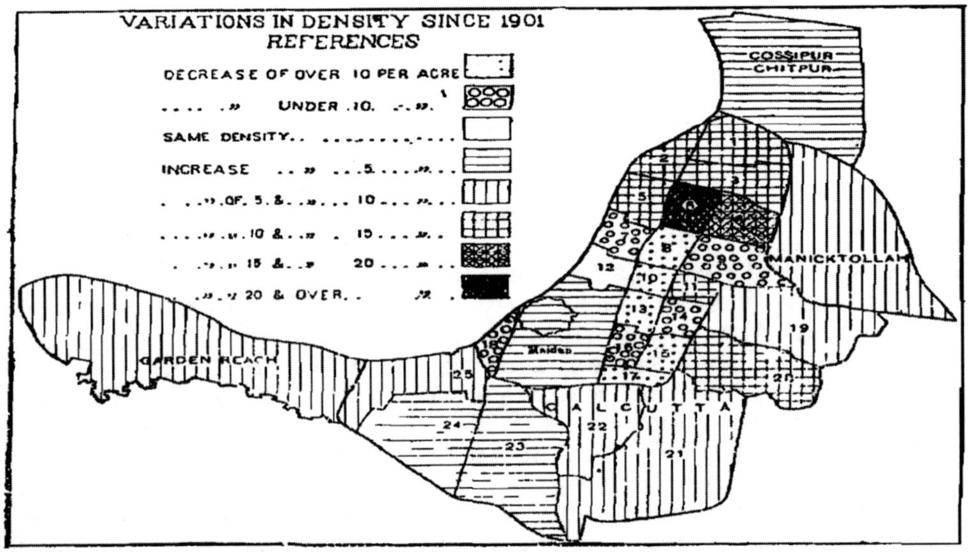

28. There are thus two main factors which have tended to reduce density during the last ten years, viz., (1) the demolition of *bastis* in the interests of sanitation, and (2) the substitution of shops, warehouses and business premises for huts closely huddled together. The operation of the first of these factors may be illustrated by the decrease in Ward No. 8 (Kalutola), which in 1901 had an average of 282 persons per acre. Since then the acquisition of land for public buildings and the improvement of *bastis* have forced many of the cooly population to move out. The resident population has consequently decreased by 10 per cent.; though still the most densely populated ward in the city, it now supports only 255 persons per acre. The operation of the second factor may be illustrated by the case of Jorabagan, which in 1901 held, with Jorasanko, second place in order of density. This is one of the commercial quarters, where dwelling-houses have been replaced by shops, besides which *bastis* have been obliterated It has grown by only 6 per cent. and is now third on the list, whereas Jorasanko has advanced twice as rapidly and, with 227 persons per acre, is the most densely populated ward next to Kalutola.

In seven central wards, which in 1901 had a density of 100 persons per acre and over, the pressure of the people on the limited space available for them has been reduced, while in six wards to the north it has increased. The European wards have also been opened out, and the density, though high, diminished considerably. All the suburban wards, in which there is room for expansion, have benefited by the overflow of the displaced population, and in all of them there has, consequently, been an increase in the mean density.

HOUSES.

29. Statistics of the number of occupied houses in Calcutta and the Suburbs will be found in Table 1 in the Volume of Tables, while information regarding the average number of persons per house and of houses per acre at each of the last four

censuses is contained in Subsidiary Table II at the end of this chapter. Comparison of the results obtained at this census and previous enumerations is however, rendered impossible by changes in the definition of houses for census purposes. In 1891 each *bari*, or collection of houses in a single compound, was treated as a house, but at the census of 1901 the house was defined as the dwelling place of one or more families, having a separate independent entrance from the common way. The result of the definition being changed was that in 1901 the number of occupied houses in the municipal area of Calcutta (120,469) was nearly double that recorded at the previous census (67,528). At this census it was decided to adopt the municipal premise as the limit, the advantage of this course being that, as all municipal premises are numbered, it facilitated work and prevented any buildings being omitted. At the same time, in *bastis* which may contain a score or several scores of huts, all covered by one municipal number), subsidiary numbers were given to those huts which were inhabited by separate families. The practice, however, was not uniform, for in some cases the *basti* number, and in others the hut number, was taken as the unit. The effect of this procedure is briefly that the houses entered in the table of statistics represent occupied municipal premises, except in the case of *bastis*, where they represent sometimes the whole *basti* and sometimes the individual hut. The "house" therefore is an artificial unit, corresponding neither to the family nor the residential house, for the municipal premise includes not only apartments occupied by different families in the same building, but also unconnected buildings In the Suburbs the municipal premise was also taken to represent a census house, but in certain areas other definitions had to be adopted. In the Port Commissioners' property, Fort William and the Maidan the "house" was the inhabited building to which a separate number was given, and in the Port and Canals it represented an occupied vessel.

30. In order to obtain information regarding the number of families and their accommodation, a special form of house list was adopted, in which particulars were entered of families, the number of persons in each family and the number of inhabited rooms occupied by them (excluding rooms used for non-residential purposes, such as shops, godowns, etc.) These lists were filled up during the preliminary enumeration, and statistics have been compiled from them for 719,000 persons, forming 151,000 families and living in 287,000 rooms. The results are given in Subsidiary Table III at the end of this chapter.* It will be seen that, approximately, each family consists of five persons, who have to find accommodation in two rooms. The largest families are found in Hastings, the average being nearly 7, and the smallest in Park Street, a European ward, where the mean is only 3. This latter ward also, as might be expected, has the greatest room space. There is least accommodation in Jorabagan, a densely populated ward, where there is only one room for every family of four to five persons.

* The averages have been shown in decimals to one point, a method which seems *primâ facie* absurd when applied to persons and rooms, but it is impossible to express the variations in different parts of the city in any other way.

SUBSIDIARY TABLE I.—VARIATION IN RELATION TO DENSITY SINCE 1872.

WARDS.	PERCENTAGE OF VARIATION, INCREASE (+) OR DECREASE (−).				Net variation, 1872 to 1911.	MEAN DENSITY PER ACRE.				
	1901 to 1911.	1891 to 1901.	1881 to 1891.	1872 to 1881.		1911.	1901.	1891.	1881.	1872.
CALCUTTA WITH SUBURBS ...	*+ 9·9*	*+23·8*	*+10·1*	*− 3·1*	*+ 44·6*	*39*	*35*	*29*	*26*	*27*
CALCUTTA	*+ 5·7*	*+24·3*	*+11·4*	*− 3·3*	*+ 41·6*	*44*	*41*	*33*	*30*	*31*
MUNICIPAL AREA	*+ 6·3*	*+ 24·7*	*+ 12·5*	*− 5·6*	*+ 40·7*	*72*	*68*	*54*	*48*	*51*
Ward No. 1, Shampukur	+ 13·1	+ 27·1	+ 29·4	− 1·2	+ 83·8	130	115	90	70	71
,, ,, 2, Kumartoli	+ 9·7	+ 13·3	+ 13·6	− 24·5	− 2·8	152	139	123	118	157
,, ,, 3, Bartala	+ 8·8	+ 37·8	+ 25·9	− 3·3	+ 82·5	136	125	90	72	74
,, ,, 4, Sukea Street ...	+ 14·5	+ 20·7	+ 42·7	− 3·5	+ 92·2	150	131	109	78	78
,, ,, 5, Jorabagan	+ 6·2	+ 25·2	+ 7·9	− 7·1	+ 33·4	214	202	161	149	161
,, ,, 6, Jorasanko	+ 12·4	+ 27·2	+ 26·9	− 8·9	+ 65·3	227	202	159	125	138
,, ,, 7, Barabazar	− 3·4	+ 52·9	− 0·6	− 11·6	+ 29·7	141	146	95	96	108
,, ,, 8, Kalutola	− 9·6	+ 24·4	+ 7·3	− 6·9	+ 12·4	255	282	227	211	227
,, ,, 9, Muchipara	− 1·2	+ 29·6	+ 13·5	− 0·1	+ 45·2	138	139	108	95	95
,, ,, 10, Bowbazar	− 7·5	+ 19·3	+ 4·8	− 8·1	+ 6·2	170	184	154	147	160
,, ,, 11, Paddapukur	+ 6·8	+ 35·3	+ 1·2	+ 0·1	+ 46·3	181	169	125	124	123
,, ,, 12, Waterloo Street ...	− 0·3	+ 6·2	+ 2·5	+ 1·4	+ 10·2	30	30	28	27	27
,, ,, 13, Fenwick Bazar ...	− 8·9	+ 10·0	+ 9·5	− 3·3	+ 6·2	148	163	148	135	140
,, ,, 14, Taltola	− 0·4	+ 10·4	+ 12·1	− 3·9	+ 18·4	162	163	148	132	137
,, ,, 15, Collinga	− 32·2	+ 26·9	+ 11·6	− 7·3	− 10·9	64	94	74	66	71
,, ,, 16, Park Street ...	− 13·4	+ 32·3	− 7·0	+ 8·8	+ 15·9	35	40	30	32	30
,, ,, 17, Baman Bustee (Victoria Terrace).	− 42·7	+ 18·6	− 24·9	− 6·7	− 52·4	24	43	36	48	51
,, ,, 18, Hastings	− 6·2	+ 22·8	− 5·8	− 0·7	+ 7·7	51	55	45	47	48
,, ,, 19, Entally	+ 16·7	+ 14·0	+ 25·9	− 1·3	+ 65·3	41	35	31	24	25
,, ,, 20, Beniapukur	+ 34·3	+ 22·5	+ 21·8	− 6·9	+ 86·7	46	34	28	23	25
,, ,, 21, Ballygunge—Tollygunge.	+ 46·8	+ 19·2	+ 11·8	− 12·5	+ 71·3	19·3	13·1	11·0	9·8	11·2
,, ,, 22, Bhawanipore	+ 9·9	+ 16·6	+ 12·1	+ 2·4	+ 47·0	67	61	52	47	45
,, ,, 23, Alipore	+ 11·5	+ 19·7	+ 10·2	− 30·8	+ 1·7	15·9	14·2	11·9	10·8	16·6
,, ,, 24, Ekbalpore	+ 1·2	+ 40·9	− 3·3	− 12·2	+ 21·0	23·7	23·4	16·6	17·2	19·6
,, ,, 25, Watganj	+ 15·5	+ 41·3	− 3·9	+ 21·2	+ 20·2	60	52	37	38	32
Fort William and Maidan	+ 3·25	− 8·0	+ 8·4	+ 34·5	+ 77·6	3·4	2·5	2·8	2·6	1·9
Port	− 9·7	+ 12·0	− 5·7	+ 69·3	+ 61·4	3·8	4·2	3·7	4·0	2·3
Canals	− 26·6	+111·6	− 30·1	+ 70·8	+ 85·4	12·1	16·4	7·7	11·1	6·5
SUBURBS	*+45·3*	*+15·8*	*+ 0·7*	*− 9·0*	*+ 66·1*	*23*	*16*	*14*	*13*	*14*
Cossipur-Chitpur	+ 18·2	+ 29·7	+ 19·5	+ 3·6	+ 89·9	23	20	15	13	12
Manicktollah	+ 66·0	+ 15·0	− 41·5	− 10·9	− 0·4	5	15	13	22	25
Garden Reach	+ 60·6	+ 1·0	+124·2	+ 34·5	+ 389·3	21	13	13	6	4

SUBSIDIARY TABLE II.—PERSONS PER HOUSE AND HOUSES PER ACRE.

WARDS.	Average number of persons per house.				Average number of houses per acre.			
	1911.	1901.	1891.	1881.	1911.	1901.	1891.	1881.
CALCUTTA WITH SUBURBS	*17*	*6·57*	...	...	*2*	...	...	...
CALCUTTA	*20*	*6·74*	...	..	*2*	..	...	...
MUNICIPAL AREA	*22*	*6·7*	*9·61*	...	*3*	...	...	
Ward No. 1, Shampukur	18	6	8·93	8·25	7	33·88	11·01	10·54
,, ,, 2, Kumartoli	18	6	9·98	9·59	9	24·56	12·89	14·90
,, ,, 3, Bartala	19	7	8·40	8·49	7	32·39	11·45	11·04
,, ,, 4, Suken Street	22	6	9·63	8·15	7	44·02	11·78	10·62
,, ,, 5, Jorabagan	27	8	14·4	13·31	8	27·16	11·79	12·29
,, ,, 6, Jorasanko	21	7	12·89	10·33	11	29·75	14·49	13·92
,, ,, 7, Barabazar	24	10	9·95	12·22	6	31·04	12·12	12·69
,, ,, 8, Kalutola	34	7	16·57	16·89	8	43·52	16·0	14·38
,, ,, 9, Muchipara	19	7	11·45	11·84	7	43·03	10·33	13·49
,, ,, 10, Bowbazar	20	9	14·62	14·70	8	24·88	10·7[illegible]	11·99
,, ,, 11, Paddapukur	18	7	8·77	11·35	10	25·18	16·16	1[illegible]·98
,, ,, 12, Waterloo Street	17	8	12·48	16·43	2	5·36	2·38	1·[illegible]
,, ,, 13, Fenwick Bazar	21	5	15·82	13·95	7	27·64	9·83	10·75
,, ,, 14, Taltola	22	6	12·05	12·60	7	30·55	11·89	10·8[illegible]
,, ,, 15 Collinga	20	5	10·40	11·66	3	17·10	8·45	6·39
,, ,, 16, Park Street...	26	7	19·25	21·32	1	5·95	1·56	1·24
,, ,, 17, Baman Bustee (Victoria Terrace)	20	10	8·23	15·69	1	4·44	3·14	1·92
,, ,, 18, Hastings	26	5	18·82	8·74	2	12·69	2·45	10·21
,, ,, 19, Ertally	31	6	7·69	7·06	1	5·80	4·37	3·84
,, ,, 20, Beniapukur	24	5	5·68	6·75	2	6·19	5·27	3·67
,, ,, 21, Ballygunge-Tollygunge	16	4	5·83	...	1	3·33	2·17	
,, ,, 22, Bhawanipore	15	5	7·07	7·18	4	12·75	7·89	5·23
,, ,, 23, Alipore	26	5	6·23	6·91	1	2·90	2·06	1·77
,, ,, 24, Ekbalpore	41	4	6·10	..	1	5·61	2·81	..
,, ,, 25, Watganj	34	6	8·52	...	2	11·35	4·63	
Fort William and Maidan	7	7	...	...	1	...	...	...
Fort	8	8	..	...	0·4	...	...	...
Canals	5	5		...	2	...	...	
SUBURBS	*8*	*5*	...	...	*3*	*2·78*	...	...
Cossipure—Chitpur	8	7	6·0	3·27	3	2·65	2·32	2·62
Manicktollah	9	5	5·9	...	3	2·77	2·13	..
Garden Reach	9	4	...	...	2	2·96	..	..

SUBSIDIARY TABLE III.—FAMILIES AND THEIR ACCOMMODATION.

Locality.	Total number of families.	Total number of persons.	Number of persons per family.	Total number of inhabited rooms.	Number of rooms per family.	Number of persons per room.
CALCUTTA MUNICIPAL AREA	*151,963*	*718,997*	*4·8*	*287,006*	*1·9*	*2·5*
Ward No. 1, Shampukur	9,693	46,283	4·8	21,571	2·2	2·2
„ „ 2, Kumartoli	5,949	29,619	5·0	13,183	2·2	2·3
„ „ 3, Bartala	8,768	45,046	5·1	19,371	2·2	2·3
„ „ 4, Sukea Street	8,562	42,876	5·0	19,000	2·2	2·3
„ „ 5, Jorabagan	10,063	45,509	4·5	10,313	1·0	4·4
„ „ 6, Jorasanko	6,919	46,621	6·7	21,981	3·2	2·1
„ „ 7, Barabazar	4,520	24,019	5·3	7,524	1·7	3·2
„ „ 8, Kalutola	12,189	53,428	4·4	18,360	1·5	2·9
„ „ 9, Muchipara	10,645	54,145	5·0	21,960	2·0	2·5
„ „ 10, Bowbazar	4,604	21,030	4·6	8,068	1·8	2·6
„ „ 11, Paddapukur	5,436	25,784	4·7	12,143	2·2	2·1
„ „ 12, Waterloo Street	1,207	4,625	3·8	2,062	1·7	2·2
„ „ 13, Fenwick Bazar	4,684	22,091	4·7	7,506	1·6	2·9
„ „ 14, Taltola	5,206	27,284	5·2	10,603	2·0	2·6
„ „ 15, Collinga	2,250	9,357	4·2	5,160	2·2	1·8
„ „ 16, Park Street	963	2,871	3·0	2,188	2·3	1·3
„ „ 17, Baman Bustee (Victoria Terrace)	582	2,327	4·0	1,091	1·9	2·1
„ „ 18, Hastings	469	3,209	6·8	1,471	3·1	2·2
„ „ 19, Entally	8,410	37,313	4·4	12,653	1·5	2·9
„ „ 20, Beniapukur	5,846	30,381	5·2	10,575	1·8	2·9
„ „ 21, Ballygunge-Tollygunge	7,285	31,386	4·3	12,815	1·8	2·5
„ „ 22, Bhawanipore	9,008	44,120	4·9	20,645	2·3	2·1
„ „ 23, Alipore	3,133	13,757	4·4	5,368	1·7	2·6
„ „ 24, Ekbalpore	4,333	17,425	4·0	6,530	1·5	2·7
„ „ 25, Watganj	10,527	38,421	3·6	14,855	1·4	2·6

CHAPTER III.

MIGRATION.

CALCUTTA.

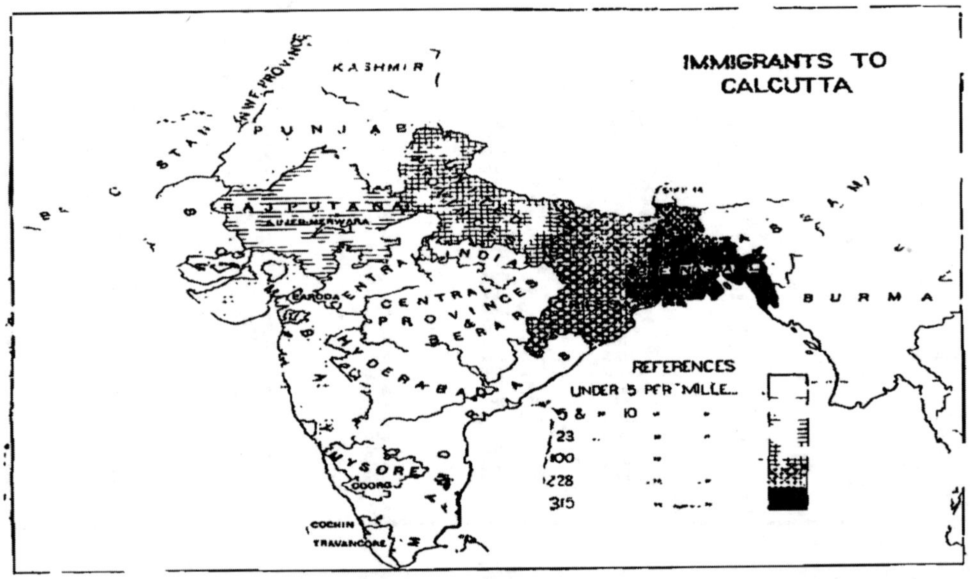

31. Nothing perhaps gives so clear an idea of the cosmopolitan character of Calcutta as the statistics of birth-place, unless it be the statistics of language. Calcutta itself is the birth-place of only three-tenths of its residents, and one-tenth come from places in the 24-Parganas. The number born elsewhere in Bengal is barely one-fifth of the population, and nearly two-fifths are immigrants from other parts of India. Those born in other Asiatic countries number 4,791, and persons of European birth 7,630, while 140 were born in Africa, 204 in America, 208 in Australasia and 31 at sea. These figures sufficiently show the heterogeneous nature of the population, and the subsequent sections of this chapter will be devoted to a more detailed discussion of the origin of its inhabitants.

32. The most noticeable feature of immigration from Bengal is the large proportion contributed by West Bengal. Nearly one-half of the Bengali immigrants come from the Burdwan Division, Hooghly sending 48,000, Midnapore 29,000, Burdwan 21,000 and Howrah 15,000. The quota of the 24-Parganas is, as might be expected, a large one, amounting to 88,000, or nearly one-third of the Bengali immigrants. This figure includes those born in the Suburbs. The remainder of the Presidency (*i.e.*, the whole of Bengal excluding the Burdwan Division, the 24-Parganas and Calcutta itself) contributes only 73,000, of whom 17,000 are natives of Dacca.

IMMIGRATION FROM BENGAL

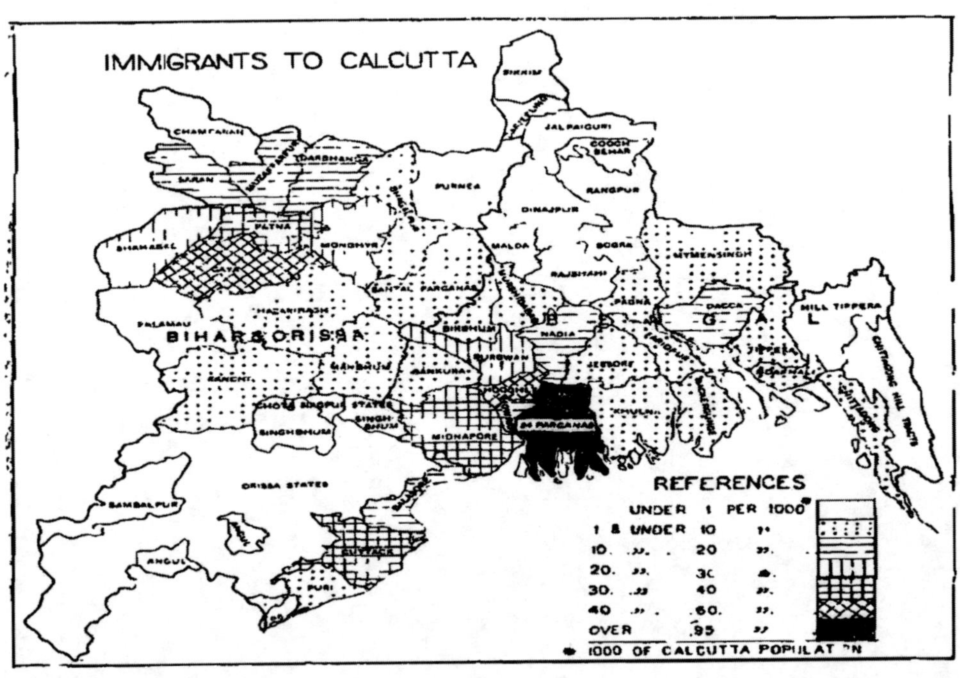

The paucity of the immigrants from districts east of Hooghly is very noticeable. Even from districts so near as Khulna, Jessore, Nadia and Murshidabad the people mostly move to other agricultural areas, and not to the metropolis: only 1 in every 12 of the persons born in these four districts who were enumerated outside their boundaries had found their way to Calcutta. Under 4,000 immigrants come from North Bengal, in spite of the facilities of railway communication, and the sum total of immigrants from the Dacca and Chittagong Divisions (36,000) is less than the number from Hooghly or even the distant district of Gaya.

The Bengal-born population of the city is actually less than in 1901 owing to the decrease in the number of those born and enumerated in it. There has been an increase of 25,000, or 9 per cent., in the number of immigrants from the Bengal districts, the greater part of which is due to a larger influx from the 24-Parganas (5,000) and the Burdwan Division (12,000). The stream of immigration from other parts of the Presidency is growing no stronger.

EMIGRATION TO BENGAL.

33. The number of persons born in Calcutta who have made their homes in other parts of Bengal is only 57,000. Many of these are of course persons who were born in Calcutta while their parents were temporary sojourners there. There being a constant flow of people between the city, the suburbs and villages in the neighbourhood, the largest number is naturally found in the 24-Parganas and then in Howrah. These two districts between them account for 48,000 of the Calcutta-born emigrants, or over four-fifths of the total number. It is noticeable that since 1901 the number of emigrants to Howrah has risen by 7,000 and to the 24-Parganas by 23,000. In the case of the latter district, however, part of the increase is fictitious, as it is due to persons who were born in Garden Reach returning Calcutta as their place of birth. There has also been a growth in the number of emigrants from these two districts, but it is not sufficient to counterbalance the increase in the number of emigrants, the result of the balance of migration being as shown in the margin.

Excess of immigrants from over emigrants to—	1911.	1901.
Howrah ...	5,000	9,000
24-Parganas ...	51,000	63,000

BIHAR AND ORISSA AND THE UNITED PROVINCES.

34. Calcutta gains mainly by the movement of the people from the west and north-west, and especially from Bihar and Orissa and the United Provinces, the immigrants from which outnumber those who have come into the city from Bengal.

The aggregate of immigrants from Bihar and Orissa alone, viz., 204,000, exceeds by 10,000 the number hailing from the districts of Bengal, excluding the 24-Parganas. Altogether 155,000 are recruited from Bihar, 41,000 from Orissa and 9,000 from Chota Nagpur and the Sonthal Parganas. The districts from which the greatest number come are Gaya (41,000), Patna (29,000) and Cuttack (27,000). The influx from Bihar and Orissa, large as it was in 1901, has now attained still greater dimensions. The actual rise in the number of immigrants amounts to 39,000, or 24 per cent., to which the districts shown in the margin contribute most largely. Those born in the United Provinces number 90,000, or double the number of immigrants from Eastern Bengal. Of these, over a third are drawn from the four districts of Benares (12,000), Azamgarh (9,000), Ghazipur (9,000) and Jaunpur (7,000). Immigration from the United Provinces shows no tendency to expand, the number of imigrants being 719 less than in 1901.

Districts.	1911.	1901.
Gaya ...	41,221	36,853
Shahabad ...	20,866	16,090
Monghyr ...	18,283	9,713
Muzaffarpur	17,369	12,831
Darbhanga ..	9,014	6,064
Cuttack ...	27,367	18,469
Balasore ...	12,491	7,182

OTHER PARTS OF INDIA.

35. The largest supply of immigrants from other parts of India comes from Rajputana, chiefly from Jaipur (8,000) and Bikanir (7,000). Emigration to Calcutta from this area is clearly growing in popularity, the number rising from 15,000 to 21,000 in the last ten years. Considerable increases are also recorded for Assam, the Central Provinces, Madras, Bombay and the Punjab. The Punjab sends

9,000, of whom nearly a third are natives of Delhi, Lahore and Amritsar; and Assam 5,000, of whom 2,390 were born in Sylhet. Bombay contributes as many as Assam, while Madras and the Central Provinces are each responsible for 3,000, and the Central India Agency for a little over 1,000, mainly from Gwalior.

OTHER ASIATIC COUNTRIES.

36. There are nearly 5,000 immigrants from other Asiatic countries, half of whom come from China. The Chinese colony is growing steadily by the accession of new-comers, the addition since 1901 amounting to 640, which has brought up the number of those born in China to 2,349. There are 758 emigrants from Nepal and 542 from Afghanistan, but no other Asiatic country contributes over 400.

EUROPE.

37. Practically every country in Europe is represented in the returns, the aggregate being 7,630, of whom 6,571 were born in the United Kingdom, viz., 5,111 in England and Wales, 1,034 in Scotland, 424 in Ireland and 2 in the Channel Islands and Isle of Man. Next to the United Kingdom, most of the Europeans come from Germany (256), Austria-Hungary (142 , France (114) and Russia (112). Russia alone of the European countries sends more females than males; nearly half the women born there who have come to Calcutta are prostitutes.

DISTRIBUTION BY WARDS.

38. The marginal map shows the distribution of immigrants by wards. Those in which they congregate most thickly are Barabazar, Waterloo Street, Alipore, which has a cantonment for native troops, and Watganj, which contains the docks. In each of these wards more than nine-tenths of the population are foreign-born. The proportion rises above four-fifths in Jorabagan, Park Street, Baman Bustee and Bhawanipore; and the minimum is reached in Beniapukur, where a little more than half the inhabitants are natives of Calcutta, *i.e.*, were born and reside there. Subsidiary Table *III* at the end of this chapter shows the principal countries in which the immigrants enumerated in each ward were born. The Bengalis are most numerous in Shampukur and Muchipara, while the Biharis gather in greatest strength in Kalutola, Muchipara and Entally. Jorabagan, Barabazar, Kalutola and Watganj contain more of the men from the United Provinces than any other of the wards. The Bombay immigrants apparently find Barabazar the most congenial locality, while the Punjabis divide themselves, for the most part, between that ward and Kalutola. By far the greater number of those hailing from the Central Provinces, Central India and Rajputana are found in Jorabagan and Barabazar, while half the Chinese have established themselves in Kalutola.

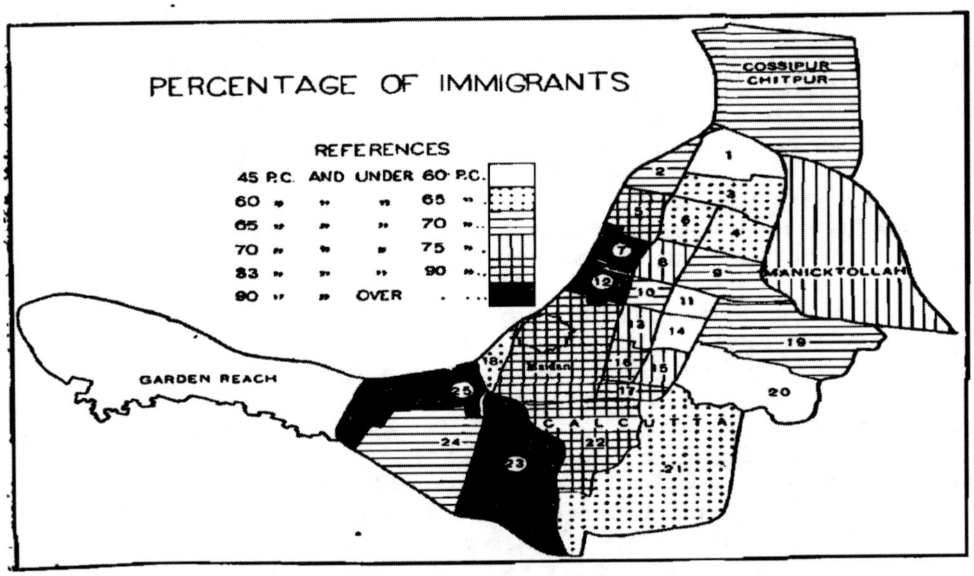

CONSTITUTION OF THE IMMIGRANT POPULATION.

39. A special return, which has been prepared of the ages and occupations of 26 large and representative castes among the immigrant population, yields some interesting information regarding the character of the foreign-born population of Calcutta. The aggregate number dealt with is 290,000,

and of the districts from which they are drawn 9 are in Bengal, 9 in Bihar and Orissa, 4 in the United Provinces, and 2 in Rajputana. The figures may therefore be taken as typical of the immigrant population. There are only 2 female to every 5 male immigrants; over two-thirds of the latter are actual workers, but only one-fourth of the females are actually engaged in any occupation. Prostitutes alone account for one-fourth of the female workers, and their number is equal to one-seventh of the women of adult age. Altogether 15 per cent. of both sexes are under 15 years of age. Half the women and two-thirds of the men are adults, *i.e.*, aged 15 to 40: at this age period there are three males to every female. Trade engages the energies of 19 per cent. of the male workers, while 14 per cent. are employed in domestic service, 13 per cent. are day-labourers and 7 per cent. are clerks. Domestic service accounts for the largest proportion of female workers, viz., 42 per cent., and then come prostitutes with 25 per cent. Brahmans represent nearly one-fifth of the total number of immigrants, and the Kayasths are the next largest caste, representing about one-seventh. The aggregate of the three trading castes of Agarwala, Mahesri and Subarnabanik is equal to only 5 per cent., and is less than that returned for four of the lower castes, viz., Chamar, Chasi Kaibartta, Goala and Kahar. The returns for the Brahmans show to what an extent the absence of home surroundings loosens the ties of orthodoxy and tradition; for one-fifth of the male workers are traders and one-seventh are clerks: there are nearly as many Brahman as Kayasth clerks. Four per cent of the priestly class are day-labourers or coolies, and only 9 per cent. returned priesthood as their occupation or means of livelihood.

40. The distribution of some occupations among the immigrant castes is somewhat surprising. The Brahmans and Kayasths, as might be expected, form the majority of clerks and Government servants, but it is, at first sight, a little astonishing that these two castes should form nearly a third of the traders and actually outnumber the members of all the five mercantile castes, viz., Agarwalas, Gandhabaniks, Maheshris, Subarnabaniks and Telis, taken together. Domestic servants are chiefly recruited from among Brahmans, Chamars, Chasi Kaibarttas, Goalas, Kayasths and Kahars. Nearly two-thirds are Brahmans, Goalas and Kahars, and all but the Chamars are clean castes: the presence of the latter in the list shows how lax the people of Calcutta have become in their choice of servants. The chief castes from which maid-servants are drawn are the Chasi Kaibarttas and Kayasths, who, between them, account for a third of the total number. Work in mills and factories provides employment for nearly all the 26 castes, except the trading castes of Agarwala, Gandhabanik, Mahesri and Subarnabanik, the Baidyas, Sunris and Dhobas. Nearly a fifth of the workers in the mills are Chamars, who also furnish about one-third of the carters. The Oriya Khandaits—or men who claim to be Khandaits—are most strongly represented among the day-labourers and coolies, and the Baishnabs and Brahmans among the beggars. Nearly a sixth of the foreign-born prostitutes are Chasi Kaibarttas, and nearly as many are Baishnabs: other castes supplying a large number of these unfortunate women are the Brahmans, Kayasths and Sadgops. Nearly all the *darwans* are Brahmans and Rajputs from Bihar and the United Provinces; the cobblers and shoe-makers are all Chamars and Muchis, seven-tenths of whom come from Monghyr, Patna and Shahabad. The gardeners are mostly immigrants from Cuttack, who claim to be Khandaits, and a considerable proportion of the syces are Dosadhs from Bihar.

SUBURBS.

41. In Garden Reach less than half the population is foreign-born, but in Cossipur-Chitpur the proportion rises to two-thirds and in Manicktollah to three-fourths. The term "foreign-born," it may be explained, has a different meaning, as applied to these municipalities, from that which it bears in the case of Calcutta. An immigrant in Calcutta means a person born outside the city. An immigrant in Cossipur-Chitpur and Manicktollah means a person

born outside the 24-Parganas, *i.e.*, either in Calcutta or any other part of India, Asia, Europe, etc.; but in Garden Reach it means a person born in any place but Calcutta and the 24-Parganas. The different classification adopted for the latter municipality is due to the fact that a large number of those born in Garden Reach returned themselves as born in Calcutta, and it is not possible to differentiate between them. Taking the Suburbs as a whole, we find that 45 per cent. of the population were born either in Calcutta or the 24-Parganas. The remainder of Bengal accounts for 25,000 immigrants, nearly two-thirds of whom come from the Burdwan Division. Of those who have been recruited from outside Bengal, all but 3,000 are natives either of Bihar and Orissa (26,000), or the United Provinces (27,000). Of these 20,000 come from Bihar, the districts with the largest shares being Shahabad (5,000) and Gaya (4,000). Altogether 5,000 come from Orissa, nearly 4,000 of whom are natives of Cuttack.

SUBSIDIARY TABLE I.—Immigration (Actual figures).

Enumerated in—	Born in (000's omitted):— Calcutta and Suburbs.			Contiguous districts of Bengal.			Other parts of Bengal.			Other Provinces.			Outside India.		
	Total.	Male.	Female.	Total.	Male.	Female.	Total.	Male.	Female.	Total.	Male.	Female.	Total.	Male.	Female.
1	2	3	4	5	6	7	8	9	10	11	12	13	14	15	16
Calcutta	257	137	120	104	58	46	179	125	54	344	278	66	13	10	3
Suburbs	33	18	15	36	19	17	22	13	9	55	39	16	·5	·4	·1

SUBSIDIARY TABLE II.—Proportional migration to and from Calcutta and Suburbs.

Locality.	Number per mille of actual population of— Immigrants.			Emigrants.			Number of females to 100 males. Immigrants.		Emigrants.	
	Total.	From contiguous districts.	From other places.	Total.	To contiguous districts.	To other places.	From contiguous districts.	From other places.	To contiguous districts.	To other places.
1	2	3	4	5	6	7	8	9	10	11
Calcutta	714	116	598	98	53	45	78	30	90	77
Suburbs	779	247	532	...	...	...	90	47	...	..

Statistics of emigration from the Suburbs are not available.

SUBSIDIARY TABLE III.—DISTRIBUTION BY WARDS OF IMMIGRANTS FROM SELECTED PROVINCES AND COUNTRIES.

Born in—	Ward. I	II	III	IV	V	VI	VII	VIII	IX	X	XI	XII
Presidency and Burdwan Divisions.	38,774	22,201	36,819	23,161	20,930	36,522	7,016	21,644	37,465	12,778	20,766	593
Other districts of Bengal ...	2,216	3,441	2,581	1,770	1,433	1,604	741	1,606	5,963	1,354	1,485	68
Bihar	2,761	2,106	6,141	6,812	7,065	9,733	3,717	16,821	10,170	5,507	2,409	1,301
Orissa	2,308	2,216	2,334	1,109	1,556	3,933	687	3,982	2,561	1,340	3,426	445
Chota Nagpur	1,364	27	657	136	101	144	44	325	684	144	79	46
Bombay	15	8	12	46	265	134	2,534	632	135	334	66	88
United Provinces ..	5,063	2,478	5,506	4,006	3,221	3,961	6,861	6,712	3,901	1,997	940	1,998
Punjab, North-West Frontier Province and Afghanistan.	256	87	84	131	637	380	1,246	1,765	503	290	317	403
Central Provinces, Central India and Rajputana.	91	195	180	75	8,607	1,155	7,170	904	556	263	119	182
Madras	1	2	11	31	26	8	160	180	144	257	156	63
China	3	...	...	...	...	...	5	1,391	1	315	96	131
British Isles	...	1	6	35	31	3	103	44	183	180	19	584
Other countries in Europe .	1	...	...	3	3	...	25	35	11	32	...	151
Total ...	*52,872*	*32,762*	*54,281*	*47,315*	*49,095*	*57,582*	*30,292*	*56,673*	*62,136*	*24,011*	*29,938*	*6,049*

Born in—	Ward. XIII	XIV	XV	XVI	XVII	XVIII	XIX	XX	XXI	XXII	XXIII	XXIV	XXV
Presidency and Burdwan Divisions.	11,784	18,567	4,292	714	404	2,306	27,197	23,161	27,682	36,035	8,962	13,855	16,011
Other districts of Bengal ...	2,252	2,127	535	76	95	158	1,112	460	1,901	2,679	497	652	2,408
Bihar	8,222	6,874	3,000	1,483	717	1,036	10,465	8,955	5,374	7,814	2,556	2,826	6,658
Orissa	1,671	790	786	853	658	256	1,302	642	1,700	1,930	932	600	2,278
Chota Nagpur	39	218	41	25	15	63	1,077	161	206	528	518	135	559
Bombay	236	128	68	82	44	22	45	39	32	92	33	63	124
United Provinces	2,116	1,596	920	759	375	1,183	3,284	1,787	2,299	3,783	1,590	2,998	5,952
Punjab, North-West Frontier Province and Afghanistan.	275	247	201	106	38	110	93	168	121	257	867	148	179
Central Provinces, Central India and Rajputana.	175	81	40	42	12	63	140	50	26	197	127	293	416
Madras	349	247	102	51	42	113	43	31	73	209	72	52	281
China	135	...	...		1	6	16	2	1	2	7	...	10
British Isles	519	167	358	631	387	106	91	47	282	398	140	30	102
Other countries in Europe ..	155	66	89	78	59	18	9	5	52	51	8	27	19
Total ...	*27,951*	*31,138*	*11,026*	*4,901*	*2,907*	*5,542*	*44,860*	*37,408*	*39,749*	*53,970*	*16,011*	*21,686*	*34,897*

CHAPTER IV.

RELIGION.

CALCUTTA.

General Results.

42. The Hindus number 604,853 and represent a little over two-thirds of the population of Calcutta, while the Musalmans number 241,587, or a little over one-fourth. There are five Hindus to every two Musalmans, and their actual numerical superiority is 363,266. The Christians number 39,551 or 4 per cent., and the remaining religions are an insignificant minority. Their aggregate is barely 10,000, and none has even 2,500 adherents. As shown in the marginal statement, immigrants predominate largely over the native-born population in the case of all but the Jews and Christians. Of the former three-fifths and of the latter nearly a half were born in Calcutta. It is obvious therefore that fluctuations in numbers must be mainly due to external causes, *i.e.*, to the extent to which immigration is quickened or the reverse.

Religion.	Total number.	Number born— In Calcutta.	Number born— Outside Calcutta.	Increase or decrease since 1901.
Hindu	604,853	163,237	441,616	+ 53,391
Musalman ...	241,587	72,512	169,075	− 8,352
Christian ...	,39,551	18,446	21,105	+ 1,626
Buddhist ...	2,343	374	1,969	− 560
Jew	1,919	1,136	783	+ 30
Jain	1,797	160	1,637	+ 556
Brahmo	1,529	626	903	− 270
Confucian ...	1,033	80	953	+ 855
Sikh	932	81	851	+ 779
Zoroastrian ...	467	89	378	+ 177
Animist	56	19	37	+ 56

Hindus and Musalmans.

43. The Hindus have increased by nearly 10 per cent. since 1901, and the addition to their number accounts for the growth of the whole population of the city. Three-fifths are immigrants from Bengal, one-fifth from Bihar and Orissa and one-tenth from the United Provinces. The proportion of immigrants among the Musalmans, viz., seven-tenths, is only a little less than among the Hindus. Those who have come from Bihar and Orissa represent nearly a third of the total number, and are as numerous as the immigrants from Bengal.

It is, at first sight, a little surprising than though the proportion of immigrants in the two communities is very nearly the same, the Musalmans have sustained a loss of 8,000, or 3 per cent., while the Hindus have increased by 53,000. As a partial explanation of the difference it may be pointed out that immigration from Hindu areas is developing more rapidly than from Musalman centres. As stated in the last chapter, the increase since 1901 in the number of immigrants from the Province of Bihar and Orissa, which is mainly Hindu, is nearly four times as great as among immigrants from Bengal, where Musalmans form a majority. In a city where the death-rate far exceeds the birth-rate, a community must diminish unless there are fresh recruits to fill the vacancies caused either by death or by the return of immigrants to their homes; and it is noticeable that the influx of

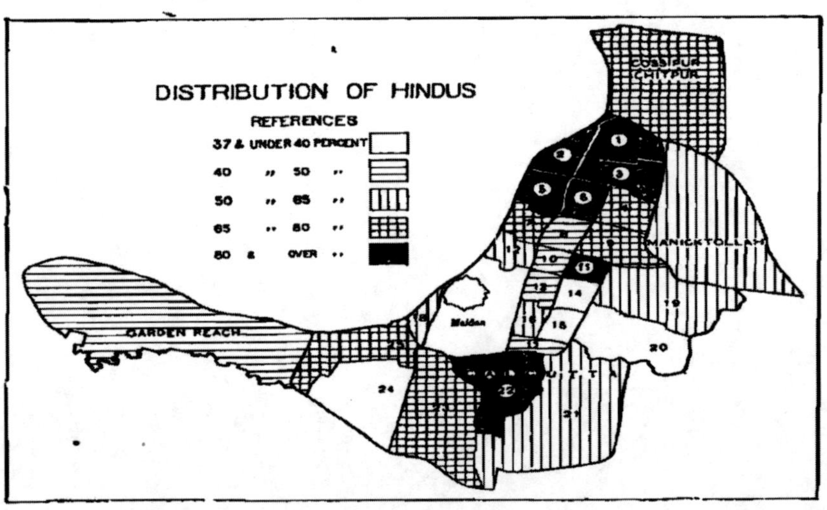

immigrants from the districts of Eastern Bengal, with their large Musalman population, has not increased. These facts, however, can only furnish an explanation of the Musalman community being stationary, and do not account for the actual decrease. This must be ascribed mainly to the overflow of Musalmans to Manicktollah and Garden Reach from adjoining wards where they are in greatest strength.

Distribution of Hindus and Musalmans

44. The maps printed in this and the preceding paragraphs illustrate graphically the distribution of the two main religious communities. The Hindus are found in greatest strength in the northern wards, viz., Shampukur, Kumartoli, Bartala, Jorabagan and Jorasanko, where they account for four-fifths or more of the population, and in Paddapukur and Bhowanipore, where the same proportion is reached. In five other wards they form two-thirds or more of the inhabitants and in four wards only does the ratio fall below two-fifths, viz., Taltollah, Collinga, Beniapukur and Ekbalpore. As the Hindus and Musalmans between them from nearly 95 per cent. of the population, it naturally follows that the relative strength of the Musalmans in different wards is more or less in an inverse ratio to that of the Hindus. They predominate in the four south-eastern wards last named and in Kalutola and Ballygunge-Tollygunge; they are a small minority in Shampukur, Kumartoli, Jorabagan, Paddapukur and Bhawanipore.

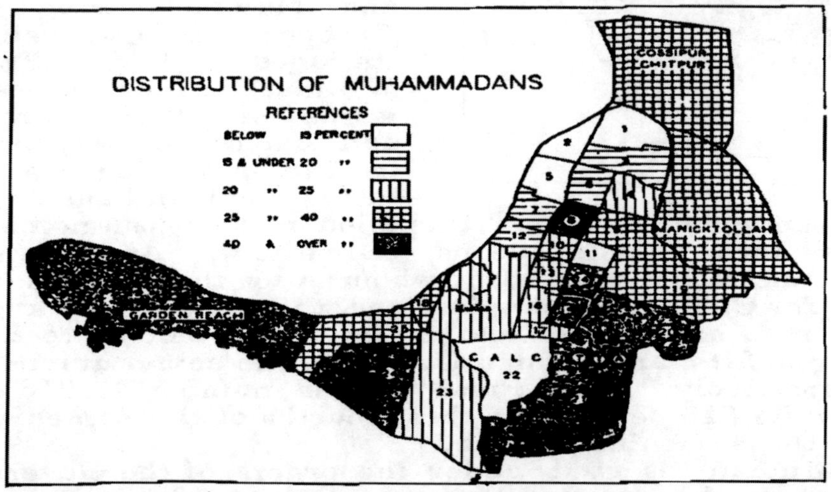

45. The Christians of Calcutta belong to three classes as shown in the margin. The variations which have occurred since 1901 will be discussed in Chapter VI, and here it is proposed only to deal with their denominations. Taking the Christian community as a whole, the number of Anglicans and Roman Catholics is almost identical, the former being 15,636 and the latter 15,692. The Baptists come third on the list with 2,521, while the Presbyterians number 1,851 and the Methodists 1,302. Of the remainder, 927 returned themselves by vague designations, such as Protestant, Dissenter, Nonconformist, etc., without specifying the particular denomination to which they had given their adherence. The Armenian Church has 638 representatives, and there are 290 Congregationalists and 250 Lutherans. Altogether 113 persons are grouped together as members of minor Protestant denominations. Of these, 39 are Adventists, 20 are Seventh-day Adventists and 33 are Evangelicals: three persons described themselves as Disciples of Christ, while the Church of India has one member.

Christians.

Class.	Number.
European and allied races ...	14,297
Anglo-Indians ...	14,177
Indian Christians ...	11,077

46. At the last census those persons who returned themselves simply as Protestants without mentioning any particular denomination, and whose denomination could not be traced by subsequent inquiries, were grouped with members of the Anglican Communion, as it was thought that the majority were members of the Church of England. It was subsequently ascertained that this was not the case, and that many Dissenters also used this vague designation. Accordingly, at this census, those who returned themselves as Protestants have been classified under the head "Protestants (Unsectarian or sect not specified)." This change of classification has affected the returns for the Anglican Communion, which now shows a decrease of 2,263 members.

The whole of the loss, however, cannot be put down to this account. As will be shown later, it is largely due to the transfer of Anglo-Indians to the Roman Catholic Church.

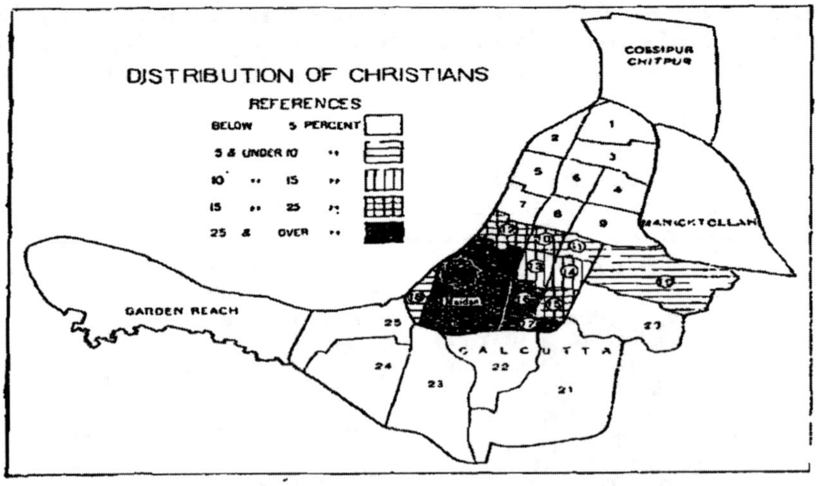

The distribution of the Christian population is sufficiently illustrated by the marginal map, from which it will be seen that they congregate most thickly in the Fort and Maidan owing to European troops being stationed in Fort William), in the European wards of Park Street and Baman Bustee, and in the adjoining wards to the north and east.

47. The term "European and allied races" is applied in the census nomenclature to Europeans, Canadians, Australians, Americans, etc., with whom also the Armenians are grouped in the returns for Christian denominations, though they are kept separate in the returns for race and age. Nearly two-thirds belong to the Anglican Communion, and one-fifth are Roman Catholics, the actual numbers being 7,939 and 3,044, respectively. The Presbyterians number 1,181, or 8 per cent. of the total, while 613 persons, or three-fourths of the Armenian community, are members of the Armenian Church.

EUROPEAN AND ALLIED RACES.

48. The term "Anglo-Indian" is used under the orders of the Government of India for those persons of mixed descent who have hitherto been designated Eurasians. Among them the representation of the Church of England and the Church of Rome is almost exactly the reverse of what it is among the Europeans, for 8,350 Anglo-Indians, or nearly two-thirds, are Roman Catholics, while 4,791, or one-third, are Anglicans. The figures are very different from those returned in 1901, the Roman Catholics being more numerous by 1,240, while the Anglicans have sustained a loss of 1,229. The close correspondence of the figures, coupled with the fact that the numerical strength of the community is almost exactly the same as it was 10 years ago, gives good reason for the belief that the Church of Rome is steadily gaining ground, whereas the Church of England is losing its hold on the domiciled community. Proportionately, the number belonging to the Church of Rome has increased by 17 per cent., while the Church of England has lost 20 per cent. of its Anglo-Indian members. Only 1,036 belong to other denominations, and nearly all of these *Baptists, Methodists or Presbyterians.*

ANGLO-INDIANS.

49. From the marginal statement showing the number of Indian Christians belonging to the principal denominations and the variations which have occurred since 1901, it will be seen that every mission has made progress except those maintained by Presbyterians and Anglicans. The decrease in the number of converts returned as Anglicans is, however, not so great as would appear from the figures owing to the change of classification of Protestants. At this census 441 persons described themselves as Protestants, who would have been grouped with Anglicans in 1901.

INDIAN CHRISTIANS.

Denominatio.	1911.	1901.	Variation.
Roman Catholic	4,298	4,246	+ 52
Anglican Communion ...	2,908	3,470	— 562
Baptist	2,015	1,028	+ 987
Methodist	696	550	+ 139
Presbyterian	395	410	— 15
Congregationalist	150	124	+ 26
Others	615	37	+ 578
Total ...	11,077	9,872	+ 1,205

The greater part of the increase of Indian Christians is due to the rapid advance made by the Baptist Church, the number of whose converts has been nearly doubled. The transfer of unspecified Protestants to another head accounts for the apparently large growth of those grouped together as "Others." Even after allowance is made for the exclusion of Protestants from the returns for Anglicans, the Church of England has to record a loss. The Methodists have gained ground, but little advance has been made either by the Church of Rome or by the Congregationalists.

MINOR RELIGIONS.

50. The Buddhists comprise a miscellany of races, such as Nepalese, Siamese, Singhaleso, Burmese, Tibetans, Japanese, and Chinese. Over half are Chinese immigrants, while 94 are Japanese (chiefly prostitutes), and 362 are Maghs from Chittagong. The Confucians are Chinese almost to a man; in the Chinese colony there are three followers of Buddha to two followers of Confucius. The Jews are mainly domiciled in Calcutta, three-fifths being born within the city limits; they are the only section of the population with an excess of females. Among the Brahmos there is only a slight disparity of the sexes, but in all other cases males are largely in excess. There has been a decrease in the number of those returned as Brahmos. The explanation is probably that those advanced thinkers whose beliefs and practices depart from the standard of Hindu orthodoxy find kindred spirits in the metropolis and feel no necessity to to renounce Hinduism. They may hold the same doctrines as the Brahmos, but do not join the Brahmo Samaj or proclaim themselves Brahmos. On the other hand, now that greater tolerance is shown to the heterodox, those who threw in their lot with the Brahmos are rejoining the main body of Hindus under such designations as Theistic Hindu or Neo-Hindus. Three-fourths were returned as Brahmo by caste as well as by religion, thereby showing that they have renounced the caste system; practically all the remainder are Kayasths and Baidyas. The other religions returned called for no special remarks. The Zoroastrians are Parsi immigrants, and the Sikhs mainly sepoys and traders from up-country. Most of the Jains are Marwari merchants from Rajputana, while the Animists are chiefly Oraons and Santals.

SUBURBS.

51. Two-thirds of the suburban residents are Hindus, their proportion to the total population being 47 per cent. in Garden Reach, 61 per cent. in Manicktollah and 71 per cent. in Cossipur-Chitpur. As the population is almost exclusively Hindu or Musalman, the corresponding ratios for Musalmans are the reverse, being 52 per cent., 38 per cent. and 27 per cent., respectively. While the Musalman population of Calcutta has declined by 8,000, that of the suburbs has increased by nearly 21,000, more than half of the net gain being registered in Manicktollah. The growth of the Musalman community is actually little less than that of Hindus, but proportionately far more. The greater part is undoubtedly due to immigration from outside districts, but there has also been an overflow from the adjoining wards of Calcutta. As shown in the margin, the Musalmans born in Calcutta and enumerated in the suburbs outnumber the Hindus except in Cossipur-Chitpur. This is the most distinctively Hindu of the three suburban towns and has naturally less attractions for the followers of the Prophet. Its boundary marches with the more purely Hindu wards of Calcutta, whereas the other two municipalities are contiguous to Musalman wards. Other religions are but sparsely represented, the aggregate for all three towns being only 1,202.

TOWN.	INCREASE, 1910-11.			
	Hindu.		Musalman.	
	Actual.	Per cent.	Actual.	Per cent.
Cossipur-Chitpur	5,376	18	1,691	15
Manicktollah	10,129	44	11,144	116
Garden Reach	9,105	75	7,927	50
Total ..	24,610	38	20,762	57

ENUMERATED IN—	BORN IN CALCUTTA.	
	Hindu.	Musalman.
Cossipur-Chitpur	1,618	403
Manicktollah	4,5 2	5,285
Garden Reach	7,383	14,543
Total ...	18,508	20,231

SUBSIDIARY TABLE I.—General distribution of the population of Calcutta by religion.

Religion.	Actual number in 1911.	Proportion per 10,000 of population. 1911	1901	1891	Variation per cent. (Increase + Decrease —). 1901-1911.	1891-1901.	Net variation 1891-1911.
1	2	3	4	5	6	7	8
Hindu	604,853	6,750	6,505	6,516	+ 9·7	+ 24·2	+ 160,716
Brahmo	1,529	17	21	11	— 15·01	+ 154·1	+ 831
Sikh	932	10	2	4	+ 500·2	— 46·7	+ 645
Jain	1,797	20	15	7	+ 41·8	+ 151·2	+ 1,303
Buddhist	2,343	26	34	32	— 19·3	+ 32·0	+ 144
Zoroastrian	467	5	4	3	+ 61·03	+ 74·7	+ 467
Muhammadan	241,587	2,696	2,948	2,981	— 3·3	+ 23·0	+ 33,414
Christian	39,561	441	447	425	+ 4·3	+ 30·8	+ 10,554
Jew	1,919	22	23	21	+ 1·6	+ 35·02	+ 520
Confucian	1,033	12	2	...	+ 480·3	...	+ 1,033
Animist	56	1	...	...	...	...	+ 56

SUBSIDIARY TABLE II.—Local Distribution of Hindus and Muhammadans.

Name of Ward.	Hindu. Proportion per 10,000. 1911.	1901.	1891.	Percentage of variation 1891 to 1911.	Muhammadan. Proportion per 10,000. 1911.	1901.	1891.	Percentage of variation 1891 to 1911.
CALCUTTA WITH SUBURBS	*6,648*	*6,485*	......	......	*2,866*	*3,019*	......	......
CALCUTTA	*6,750*	*6,505*	*6,516*	*+24·2*	*2,696*	*2,948*	*2,891*	*+23·0*
CALCUTTA (MUNICIPAL AREA)	6,900	6,665	6,609	+ 25·7	2,561	2,822	2,914	+ 20·6
Ward No. 1, Shampukur	8,817	8,481	8,403	+ 50·9	1,157	1,505	1,593	+ 4·4
" " 2, Kumartoli	9,627	9,592	9,575	+ 25·0	363	402	419	+ 7·4
" " 3, Bartala	8,324	7,894	7,592	+ 64·4	1,622	2,059	2,361	+ 3·0
" " 4, Sukea Street	7,672	7,611	7,641	+ 38·7	2,130	2,221	2,220	+ 32·5
" " 5, Jorabagan	9,489	9,347	9,370	+ 34·7	372	448	539	— 8·1
" " 6, Jorasanko	8,359	8,221	8,172	+ 46·2	1,583	1,668	1,749	+ 25·3
" " 7, Barabazar	7,577	7,216	6,745	+ 65·9	1,793	2,082	2,564	+ 3·3
" " 8, Kalutola	4,380	4,199	4,362	+ 12·9	4,792	5,022	4,863	+ 10·8
" " 9, Muchipara	6,745	6,212	6,370	+ 35·6	2,920	3,484	3,331	+ 12·3
" " 10, Bowbazar	4,239	3,883	3,756	+ 24·5	3,522	3,735	3,914	— 0·7
" " 11, Puddapukur	8,043	8,432	8,669	+ 43·9	430	718	565	+ 10·0
" " 12, Waterloo Street ...	5,600	5,395	5,750	+ 0·6	1,536	2,170	2,417	— 34·4
" " 13, Fenwick Bazar ...	4,920	5,139	5,065	— 2·6	3,674	3,678	3,841	— 4·1
" " 14, Taltola	3,892	3,713	3,632	+ 17·8	4,820	5,161	5,379	— 1·5
" " 15, Collinga	3,736	4,093	3,892	— 17·3	3,992	4,719	4,945	— 30·5
" " 16, Park Street	5,013	4,116	4,519	+ 27·1	3,059	3,583	3,284	— 28·1
" " 17, Baman Bustee (Victoria Terrace).	4,246	5,771	5,789	— 50·2	2,013	2,069	2,632	— 48·0
" " 18, Hastings	6,323	6,325	6,373	+ 14·2	2,737	2,759	2,907	+ 8·4
" " 19, Entally	6,156	6,252	6,182	+ 35·4	3,112	3,041	3,165	+ 33·7
" " 20, Beniapukur	3,965	3,927	4,256	+ 53·3	5,624	5,784	5,492	+ 63·5
" " 21, Ballygunge-Tollygunge	5,442	5,443	5,321	+ 82·4	4,210	4,171	4,513	+ 63·3
" " 22, Bhawanipore	8,577	8,217	8,157	+ 34·7	1,056	1,524	1,603	— 15·6
" " 23, Alipore	7,579	7,643	7,162	+ 41·2	2,080	2,143	2,529	+ 9·7
" " 24, Ekbalpore	3,933	4,448	3,930	+ 42·7	5,646	5,231	5,822	+ 35·3
" " 25, Watganj	6,916	6,668	6,760	+ 67·0	2,894	3,185	3,100	+ 52·4
Fort William and Maidan ...	3,906	3,972	4,155	+ 19·6	2,344	2,602	1,721	+ 73·2
Port	2,569	2,787	4,807	— 45·9	6,839	6,123	4,666	+ 48·3
Canals	5,560	4,893	5,430	+ 51·9	4,640	5,073	4,500	+ 60·1
SUBURBS	*6,020*	*6,318*	......	......	*3,898*	*3,615*	......	.....
Cossipur-Chitpur	7,147	7,130	......	......	2,[illegible]06	2,781	...	..
Manicktollah	6,123	7,037	..		3,842	2,[illegible]37	....	......
Garden Reach	4,699	4,318	......	..	5,234	5,593	......	

SUBSIDIARY TABLE III—Christians. Number and Variations.

	Actual Number of Christians.			Variation per cent.		
	1911.	1901.	1891.	1901 to 1911.	1891 to 1901.	1891 to 1911.
CALCUTTA ...	***39,551***	***37,925***	***28,997***	**+ 4·3**	***+ 30·8***	***+ 36·4***
Ward No. 1, Shampukur ...	24	35	15	− 25·7	+ 133·3	+ 73·3
,, ,, 2, Kumartoli ...	17	5	4	+ 240·0	+ 25·0	+ 325·0
,, ,, 3, *Bartala* ...	212	150	127	+ 41·3	+ 18·1	+ 66·9
,, ,, 4, Sukea Street ...	575	568	371	+ 1·2	+ 53·1	+ 55·0
,, ,, 5, Jorabagan ...	63	59	55	+ 6·8	+ 7·3	+ 14·5
,, ,, 6, Jorasanko ...	189	209	177	− 9·6	+ 18·1	+ 6·8
,, ,, 7, Barabazar ...	480	609	561	− 21·2	+ 85·6	− 14·4
,, ,, 8, Kalutola ...	2,010	2,845	2,628	− 29·3	+ 8·3	− 23·5
,, ,, 9, Muchipara ...	1,691	1,596	1,280	+ 6·0	+ 24·7	+ 32·1
,, ,, 10, Bowbazar ...	4,240	5,181	4,320	− 18·2	+ 19·9	− 1·9
,, ,, 11, Paddapukur ...	2,623	2,337	1,559	+ 12·2	+ 49·9	+ 68·2
,, ,, 12, Waterloo Street ...	1,377	1,256	978	+ 9·6	+ 28·4	+ 40·8
,, ,, 13, Fenwick Bazar ...	3,487	3,505	2,931	− 0·5	+ 19·6	+ 19·0
,, ,, 14, Taltola ...	3,988	3,534	2,715	+ 12·8	+ 30·2	+ 46·9
,, ,, 15, Collinga ...	2,528	1,944	1,520	+ 30·0	+ 27·9	+ 66·3
,, ,, 16, Park Street ...	1,514	1,345	982	+ 12·6	+ 37·0	+ 54·2
,, ,, 17, Baman Bustee (Victoria Terrace) ...	1,141	789	616	+ 44·6	+ 28·1	+ 85·2
,, ,, 18, Hastings ...	515	407	347	+ 26·5	+ 17·3	+ 48·4
,, ,, 19, Entally ...	3,199	2,610	2,159	+ 22·6	+ 20·9	+ 48·2
,, ,, 20, Beniapukur ...	1,513	772	563	+ 96·0	+ 37·1	+ 168·7
,, ,, 21, Ballygunge-Tollygunge ...	1,194	1,034	550	+ 15·5	+ 88·0	+ 117·1
,, ,, 22, Bhawanipore ...	1,843	1,207	993	+ 52·7	+ 21·9	+ 86·2
,, ,, 23, Alipore ...	428	317	287	+ 35·0	+ 10·5	+ 49·1
,, ,, 24, Ekbalpore ...	918	675	380	+ 36·0	+ 77·6	+ 141·6
,, ,, 25, Watganj ...	739	550	291	+ 34·4	+ 89·0	+ 154·0
Fort William and Maidan ...	1,645	1,578	1,251	+ 4·2	+ 26·1	+ 31·5
Port ...	1,396	2,798	1,336	− 50·0	+ 109·1	+ 4·5
Canals ...	......	15	4	− 100·0	+ 275·0	− 100·0
SUBURBS ...	***960***	***590***	......	***+ 62·7***	......	......
Cossipur-Chitpur ...	609	338	......	+ 80·2	......	......
Manicktollah ...	164	65	......	+ 152·3	......	......
Garden Reach ...	187	187	......	......	......	......

SUBSIDIARY TABLE IV—Races and Sects of Christians (Actual numbers).

Sect.	Europeans and allied races.	Anglo-Indians.	Indians.	Total.		Variation, 1901—1911.
				1911.	1901.	
CALCUTTA.						
Anglican Communion ...	7,937	4,791	2,908	15,636	17,899	− 12·6
Armenian ...	613	13	12	638	331	+ 92·7
Baptist ...	257	249	2,015	2,521	1,572	+ 60·4
Congregationalist ...	94	46	150	290	177	+ 63·8
Greek ...	142	3	4	149	87	+ 71·3
Lutheran ...	216	2	32	250	126	+ 98·4
Methodist ...	339	267	696	1,302	1,360	− 4·3
Minor Protestant denominations ...	45	19	49	113	31	+ 264·5
Presbyterian ...	1,181	275	395	1,851	1,975	− 6·3
Protestant (unspecified) ...	336	150	441	927	20	+ 4,535·0
Quaker ...	2	...	...	2	4	− 50·0
Roman Catholic ...	3,044	8,350	4,298	15,692	14,343	+ 9·5
Salvationist ...	1	...	...	1	...	
Syrian (Romo-Syrian) ...	...	2	...	2	...	...
Sect not returned ...	15	1	57	73	...	...
Indefinite beliefs ...	75	9	20	104	...	...
Total ...	***14,297***	***14,177***	***11,077***	***39,551***	***37,925***	**+ 4·3**
SUBURBS.						
Anglican Communion ...	149	99	50	298	351	− 15·1
Armenian ...	16	...	...	16	9	+ 77·8
Baptist ...	6	3	56	65	18	+ 261·1
Greek ...	16	...	...	16	14	+ 14·3
Methodist ...	19	12	79	110	20	+ 450·0
Presbyterian ...	82	2	8	92	45	+ 104·4
Protestant (unspecified) ...	16	3	104	123	...	...
Roman Catholic ...	35	173	20	228	133	+ 71·4
Sect not returned ...	1	...	8	9	...	...
Indefinite beliefs ...	8	...	...	8	...	...
Total ...	***343***	***292***	***325***	***960***	***590***	***+ 62·7***

SUBSIDIARY TABLE V.—Distribution of Christians per mille (a) races by sect and (b) sects by race.

Sect.	Races distributed by sect.				Sects distributed by race.			
	European.	Anglo Indian.	Indian.	Total.	European.	Anglo Indian.	Indian.	Total.
Calcutta.								
Anglican Communion	555	338	262	395	508	306	186	1,000
Armenian	43	1	1	16	961	20	19	1,000
Baptist	18	18	182	64	102	99	799	1,000
Congregationalist	7	3	14	7	324	159	517	1,000
Greek	10	0·2	0·8	4	953	20	27	1,000
Lutheran	15	0·1	3	6	864	8	128	1,000
Methodist	24	19	63	33	260	205	535	1,000
Minor Protestant denominations ...	3	1	4	3	398	168	434	1,000
Presbyterian	83	19	38	47	638	149	213	1,000
Protestant (unspecified)	23	11	40	23	362	162	476	1,000
Quaker	0·1	...	...	0·1	1,000	...	...	1,000
Roman Catholic	218	589	388	397	194	532	274	1,000
Salvationist	0·1	...	...	0·03	1,000	...	...	1,000
Syrian (Romo Syrian) ...	...	0·1	...	0·1	...	1,000	...	1,000
Sect not returned	1	0·1	5	2	205	14	781	1,000
Indefinite beliefs	5	1	2	3	721	87	192	1,000
Total ...	*1,000*	*1,000*	*1,000*	*1,000*	*362*	*358*	*280*	*1,000*
Suburbs.								
Anglican Communion	434	339	154	310	500	332	168	1,000
Armenian	47	...	...	17	1,000	...	...	1,000
Baptist	17	10	172	68	92	46	862	1,000
Greek	47	...	...	17	1,000	...	...	1,000
Methodist	55	41	243	115	173	109	718	1,000
Presbyterian	239	7	25	96	891	22	87	1,000
Protestant (unspecified)	47	10	320	128	130	24	846	1,000
Roman Catholic	102	593	61	237	153	759	88	1,000
Sect not returned	3	...	25	9	111	...	889	1,000
Indefinite beliefs	9	...	...	3	1,000	...	...	1,000
Total ...	*1,000*	*1,000*	*1,000*	*1,000*	*357*	*304*	*339*	*1,000*

CHAPTER V.

SEX, AGE AND CIVIL CONDITION.

INTRODUCTORY.

52. THE statistics on which the discussion in this Chapter is based will be found in Tables VII and XIV of the volume of tables. The former table shows the distribution of the total population and of the members of each religion by age, sex and civil condition, *i.e.*, it shows the number of each sex at different age periods that are unmarried, married or widowed. The figures are given separately for each year up to 5, after which they are arranged by quinquennial groups up to 70, those who are 70 and over being grouped together. In accordance with modern statistical practice, the age 0 indicates infants under one year of age, while the first number in each age group indicates the age reached and the last number the age not yet reached. The group 5-10, for instance, includes persons who are 5 years old but not yet 10 years old, *i.e.*, those whose completed ages are either 5, 6, 7, 8 or 9 years. Table XIV contains statistics of age, sex and civil condition for selected castes, the age periods 5-12 and 12-15 being substituted for the periods 5-10 and 10-15 given in the former table.

In order to bring the discussion of the results within a reasonable compass, the more prominent features of the statistics are illustrated by proportional figures in subsidiary tables at the end of this Chapter. It will therefore be unnecessary to load the Chapter with a mass of statistical details in order to explain points which can more easily be understood by a reference to these subsidiary tables or to Tables VII and XIV.

SEX.

53. There is a great disparity of the sexes both in Calcutta and the Suburbs, there being only 475 females to every 1,000 males in the former and 632 per 1,000 in the latter. The excess of males is of course due to immigration, as such a large proportion of the new-comers are adult males, who come to the city for a short time—it may be a few years or it may be only a few months—leaving their wives and families at home. If their stay in the city extends over a considerable time, they may eventually bring their wives to Calcutta and set up house there, but it more often happens that they are content to leave them in their native village and visit them at intervals. The disproportion between the sexes is steadily increasing, as the importance of Calcutta, as a commercial and industrial centre, increases, and railway communications are extended. The operation of the latter factor is of considerable importance. Immigrants come from ever increasing distances, and are therefore less likely to go to the expense of bringing women. At the same time, the ease and cheapness with which men can return to their homes makes it easier for them to do without their wives during their stay in the city.

The above figures relate only to the persons enumerated in Calcutta, but in the natural population, *i.e.*, persons born in Calcutta and enumerated either within or outside its limits, there is also a slight deficiency of females, of whom there are roughly 9 to every 10 males.

54. The paucity of women is least pronounced in Bartala and Manicktollah to the north-east and in Ballygunge-Tollygunge, Bhawanipore and Ekbalpore to the south. In all these wards the number of females is about two-thirds that of men. Females are naturally in a small minority in the Fort (125 per mille), with its garrison of soldiers, and the minimum is reached in Waterloo Street 111 per mille, which is a ward with a small population consisting mainly of persons employed in offices and shops, among whom males are in large excess.

SEX PROPORTION BY LOCALITY.

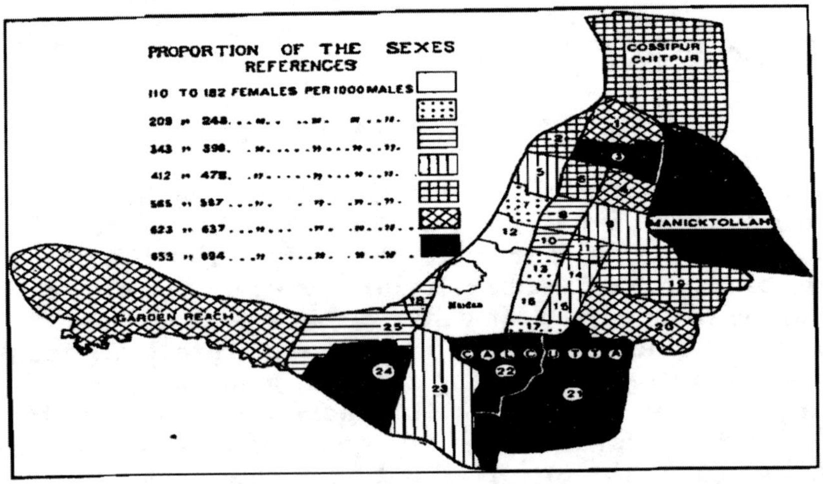

55. The Jews are the only community in which females outnumber males, though the two sexes nearly counterbalance one another among the Brahmos. From what has already been said, however, it will readily be understood that the proportion of the sexes must vary with the proportion of immigrants. A clearer idea of the sex proportions can therefore be obtained by taking the figures for the Calcutta-born population and for immigrants separately, as in the marginal statement. A study of these figures yields some interesting results.

SEX BY RELIGION.

NUMBER OF FEMALES PER 1,000 MALES.			
Religion.	Total.	Born in Calcutta.	Immigrants.
All religions	*475*	*880*	*357*
Hindu	495	864	393
Musalman	390	871	252
Christian	760	1,063	560
Buddhist	275	815	207
Jain	328	600	306
Sikh	212	976	169
Jew	1,057	1,088	1,013
Brahmo	975	1,181	854
Confucian	159	1,857	104
Parsi	593	1,067	512

In the case of immigrants, the Jews and then the Brahmos have the greatest preference for the companionship of their women-folk. Among the Jews, indeed, the two sexes are nearly equally represented in the immigrant population, a fact which *primâ facie* shows that they come to Calcutta to make permanent homes there. Among the Hindu immigrants there are 2 women to every 5 men, but among the Musalmans only 1 woman to every 4 men. The Confucian Chinese bring the fewest women, viz., 1 to every 10 men.

In the case of the Calcutta-born population it may be safely assumed that where the sexes are more or less in equal strength, it implies more or less permanent residence. Applying this criterion, we find that the communities who become domiciled in Calcutta are the Confucian Chinese, the Christians (who owe their position to the Anglo-Indians and the Indian Christians), the Jews, Parsis and Brahmos. The Chinese who were born within the city limits stand in a class by themselves, for there are approximately two women to every male. The Jains, who are mainly Marwari merchants and their employés, have the smallest proportion of permanent settlers, the ratio of males to females among them being 5 to 3.

56. The proportion of females is highest among the Baishnabs, many of whom are fallen women: there are 7 females to every 5 males. After the Baishnabs, the indigenous Bengali castes have the largest number of females, viz., in order, Tanti, Subarnabanik, Sadgop, Gandhabanik and Baidya: the proportion of females per 1,000 males among these five castes varies from 890 to 647. The antithesis is found among the Khandaits, an Oriya caste, whose men come to Calcutta to work as day labourers, gardeners, etc., until they have saved enough money to make it worth their while to return and enjoy the proceeds of their labour: among them there is only 1 woman to every 33 men.

SEX BY CASTE.

57. Statistics of the sex proportions at each quinquennial age period will be found in Subsidiary Table II. Those given in the margin sufficiently illustrate the effect of the influx of immigrants, with a large majority of of adult males, in lowering the proportion of females as age progresses.

Sex proportion by age periods and effect of births and deaths.

Number of females per 1,000 males.		
Age period.	Calcutta.	Suburbs.
0-5	937	958
0-30	504	679
30 and over	436	571

As Calcutta has such a large floating population and maintains its numbers by immigration, and not by natural growth *i e.*, by reproduction), the sex proportions at birth do not affect the general sex proportions to any great extent. From the returns of vital occurrences for the decade 1901-1910.it appears that in Calcutta, as elsewhere, more males are brought into the world than females: approximately, there are 10 male births to every 9 female births. Males being in large excess owing to immigration, the actual number of males who die is naturally far greater than the number of females; the proportion is 74 female deaths to every 100 male deaths. The excess of male deaths, however, can have little effect on the proportion of the sexes, as there is a constant influx of new comers to fill the vacancies caused by deaths in the male population.

Though more boys are born than girls, male infants, being more delicate and difficult to rear, die off more quickly than girls. In the first year of life there are only 865 deaths among the females to every 1,000 among males, and though there is not much difference between the first and fifth year, the male deaths exceed the female deaths considerably between the 5th and 10th year. After this, the excess of males among the foreign-born population begins to tell, and there is a progressive increase in the excess of male deaths. Among people between 20 and 50, the number of female deaths is under three-fifths of the male deaths, but this proportion follows the general proportion of the sexes, as shown in the margin. That there is not a closer correspondence is probably due to the fact that the age 20-50 is a critical one in a woman's life, for during it she is exposed to the dangers of childbirth.

Age period.	Number per mille.	
	Females to males.	Female deaths to male deaths.
20-30	360	573
30-40	387	539
40-50	428	550

AGE.

58. The instructions regarding the entry of age were that the number of years which each person had completed was to be entered, and that children less than one year old were to be entered as infants. The latter rule was laid down in order to prevent the number of months they had lived being entered, and so avoid the risk of that number being confused with years in compilation. Simple as these instructions are, they are beyond the capacity of the masses, who have but very vague ideas of their age, and the returns are defective in many respects. As elsewhere, there is a general tendency to return age as a multiple of 5 (*e.g.*, 10, 15, 20, etc.), and certain other features are common to the age returns of the city and the Province. The most noticeable are as follows:—

(1) The number of children returned as under 5 years of age, and especially of those aged 1, is smaller than would naturally be expected.

(2) There is a predilection for the age period 25-30, which is returned for far more persons than the period 20-25 or 30-35.

(3) There is a relative paucity of girls aged 10-15, which is probably due to a large proportion being returned as older than they really are: the number 12, it may be mentioned, is a favourite one.

(4) The figures for males are more reliable than those for females; the fluctuations in the different age periods among the latter are often remarkable.

In conclusion, it must be pointed out that immigration is a disturbing factor in the consideration of the age statistics. The population is largely a floating one, and we do not therefore get normal proportions, *i.e.*, instead of the population decreasing gradually, as age progresses and the inhabitants are depleted by death, there is actually an increase owing to the accession of new-comers.

The returns are admittedly inaccurate for children one year old, (about whose age there should *a priori* be no doubt), for their number is only about half that returned for children two years old. The explanation is partly that a large number of children still at the breast, and popularly known as infants, are returned as such and their actual age is not mentioned. The deficiency of children at this age is also partly due to the common practice of counting the current year as part of one's age, as a result of which many children who are in their second year, and who should therefore be returned as one year old, are returned as two years old.

PAUCITY OF CHILDREN.

59. One of the most noticeable features of the statistics for age is the relative paucity of children. This may be partly due to misstatement of age, but even so there is, as shown in the margin, a remarkable deficiency in the number of children under 5 compared with Bengal, in which such misstatement is equally common. Their deficiency is to be ascribed mainly to the low birth-rate; this, as explained in Chapter I, is the natural consequence of the peculiar constitution of the population, which is recruited mainly by immigration and in which males predominate. The immigrants are, moreover, mostly adults who leave their families behind, the result being that the proportion of children to the adult population (*i.e.*, persons aged 15-40) is only 27 per cent., or about one-third of that registered in Bengal as a whole (70 per cent.) The proportion to the female population of married females of the child-bearing age (*i.e.* 15 to 40 years) is, it may be added, the same as in Bengal, viz., 34 per cent., but their fecundity is very much less. A good index of the latter is afforded by the number of children under 10 to married females aged 15-40. which is 181 in Bengal, but only 132 in Calcutta and the Suburbs. The difference is probably attributable, in part at least, to the use of preventive means.

LOCALITY.	PROPORTION OF CHILDREN UNDER 5 PER 10,000 OF EACH SEX.	
	Male.	Female.
Calcutta and Suburbs	557	1,060
Bengal	1,343	1,502

INFANTILE MORTALITY.

60. The deficiency of children is also largely due to the appalling waste of infant life. Roughly, one out of every three children dies within a year of birth, and a large proportion fail to survive even the first month. The causes are several, *e.g.*, early marriage, the poor vitality of parents and the consequent debility of their offspring. Many of the mothers are poorly-fed cooly women, who continue to work to the very end of their pregnancy, with the result that they give birth to weakly, and not infrequently premature, infants, who succumb during the first few hours, days or weeks of external life. Of direct causes the principal are unskilful midwifery, disregard of the rules of hygiene and the

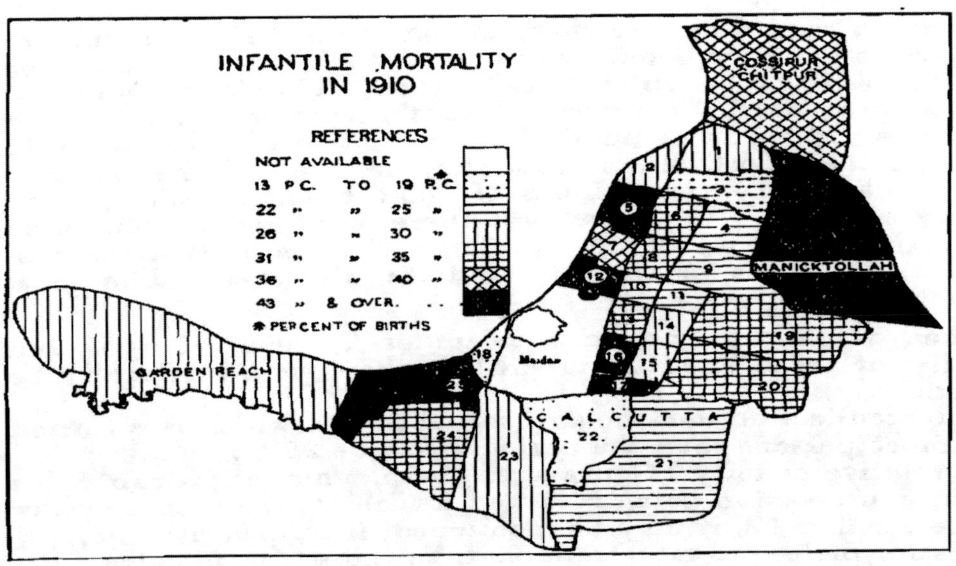

insanitary surroundings inevitable in congested areas. Lastly, the practice of cutting the umbilical cord with dirty instruments (*e.g.*, a piece of split bamboo, or a conch shell) and of applying cow-dung ashes to the freshly cut end commonly results in tetanus neonatorum and causes a very large number of deaths among healthy infants every year. On this subject I may quote the following remarks recorded by Major W. W. Clemesha, I.M.S., Sanitary Commissioner of Bengal, on the returns compiled by Dr. Pearse, Health Officer of Calcutta, for 1909, in which year more than half the deaths of children, that died within a year of birth, occurred in the first month.

61. "All who have studied the subject of infant mortality in this country recognize that the causes of infant deaths fall under two main heads. First, conditions connected with the health of parents, such as premature marriage and the prevalence of such wasting diseases as malaria, which particularly affect the well-being of the mother. The second head is equally important, viz., the extremely insanitary conditions of child birth and the appalling ignorance prevalent. The figures given by Dr. Pearse demonstrate these points to a most remarkable extent. Out of 2,700 children that die within the first month, more than 1,200, or nearly 50 per cent., come under the heads of premature birth and debility at birth These deaths obviously come under the first heading named above: probably early marriage is the preponderating factor, because malaria is comparatively rare in Calcutta. Under the second heading practically another 1,000 children die of tetanus and convulsions, diseases which are occasioned by ignorance in matters of hygiene relating to child-birth on the part of the mother and those attending to her. It appears that under these two heads about 2,200 out of 2,700 deaths can be accounted for. Grave social conditions, such as child-marriage, are things which are difficult to alter, and which the spread of education alone can hope to remedy. Deaths which are occasioned by tetanus are, however, entirely preventible. Even a little ordinary cleanliness and a little common knowledge would reduce the death-rate nearly one-half. Concerning the mortality of children between the ages of one month and one year, the causes are many and various. Bronchitis and chest troubles generally appear to account for a very large number of deaths. The children are not sufficiently clad in the cold weather, and further it is the weakly child (*i.e.*, the child of immature parents) which is most likely to contract fatal lung trouble."

THE ADULT POPULATION AND MEAN AGE.

62. In the ages of the remainder of the population the effects of migration are very clearly seen. More than half the males, and 46 per cent. of the females, are 15 to 40 years of age. After 45 there is a sharp and heavy drop in the numbers, which is obviously due to the fact that the workers leave the city for their homes and that there are few elderly immigrants to fill their places. Comparatively few men spend their declining years in the city, the proportion of men over 60 years of age to the adults (aged 15-40) being only 6 per cent., or about half what it is in Bengal. The percentage of old women, however, is double this figure, and is but little less than that for the Presidency (14 per cent.). The marginal diagram sufficiently illustrates the proportion of males and females at each age period and the difference between the age constitution of the people of Calcutta and those of Bengal.

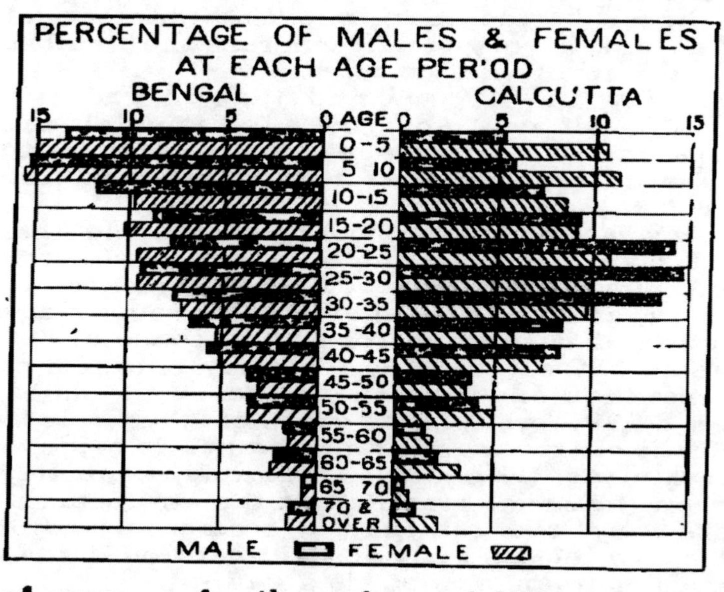

The consequence of a small proportion of young children and old persons, and of a large proportion of persons in the prime of life, is a high mean age, for mean age means merely the average age of those who are enumerated. This is 29 years for males and nearly 28 for females, whereas the figures for the whole Province are 24½ and 24, respectively.

CIVIL CONDITION.

63. As shown in the margin, a little over one-third of the males enumerated in Calcutta and the Suburbs are unmarried, but more than half of them are under 15 years of age. Less than a third of the female population are unmarried, and of these only one-tenth are over 15. The proportion of the widowed among the males is 1 in 27; but among the females one in every four is a widow. The proportions for married and unmarried persons are very different from those of Bengal as a whole, for those who have not contracted a marriage are far fewer, and those who have done so are far more numerous, than in the general population of the Presidency. The cause of this difference is that the population of Calcutta is so largely composed of adults, and that there is a relative paucity of children and old persons.

NUMBER PER 1,000 OF EACH SEX.

Civil condition.	Calcutta and Suburbs.		Bengal.	
	Male.	Female.	Male.	Female.
Unmarried ...	342	279	511	336
Married ...	621	469	454	463
Widowed ...	37	252	35	201

UNMARRIED FEMALES.

64. Another remarkable feature of the returns is the comparatively large number of unmarried females aged 20 and over that were enumerated in Calcutta. Here, however, 3,474 prostitutes, or about one-fourth of the prostitutes of that age, returned themselves as unmarried, and they alone represent half the total number of unmarried females aged 20 and over. It is on this account that the proportion of the latter to the total number of unmarried females is so high in the metropolis, viz., 9 per cent., whereas in Bengal it is only 1 per cent.

STATISTICS OF MARRIAGE.

65. Altogether 331 children under 5 years of age, and 2,903 aged 5 to 10, were returned as married. At the latter age period there are 7 young girl-wives to every 3 boy-husbands; nor need the excess of girl-wives be wondered at, for girls are married at an earlier age than boys, and it is generally considered essential that a bridegroom should be older than a bride. Between 10 and 15 half the females, but only one-tenth of the males, of Calcutta are married, while from 15 to 20 four-fifths of the former and three tenths of the latter have assumed the married state. After 20 there is a striking disparity in the proportions as shown in the margin. The number of men who remain unmarried after that age is very small, whereas the number of married women steadily decreases and that of widows rises.

NUMBER OF MARRIED PER 1,000.

Age.	Male.	Female.
20-40	787	727
40-60	888	376
60 and over ...	773	133

Taking the statistics for adult age, *i.e.*, 15—40, we find that in Calcutta 71 per cent. of the adult males and 75 per cent. of the adult females, are married. Males, however, are in large excess at this age—there are three to every female—so that married men far outnumber the married women, the proportion being 5 to 2 in the city and 5 to 3 in the Suburbs.

WIDOWERS AND WIDOWS.

66. The actual number of widowers is only 6 per cent. of the number of married men, whereas there is one widow to every two married women. The prevalence of early marriage in the Hindu community, and the bar against the remarriage of widows which exists in a large section of it account for the presence of 699 widows under 15 years of age, of whom 539 are Hindus. Nearly one-fifth of the adult women (aged 15—40), but less than one-fortieth of the adult males, are widowed: in Calcutta no less than 3,799, or 15 per cent. of the widows of this age, are prostitutes. Three-fifths of the aggregate number of widows are Hindus and only one-fifth are Musalmans, though the Musalmans remarry widows freely. The difference between the social practices of the two communities is even more clearly illustrated by the returns for women of adult age, which is also the nubile age, at which one out of every three Hindu women, but only one out of every ten Musalman women, is a widow.

SUBSIDIARY TABLE I.—General proportion of the Sexes.

Calcutta and Suburbs.	Numbers of Females to 1,000 Males.									
	1911.		1901.		1891.		1881.		1872.	
	Actual population.	Natural population.	Actual population.	Natural population.	Actual population.	Natural population.	Actual population.	Natural population.	Actual population.	Natural population.
1	2	3	4	5	6	7	8	9	10	11
Calcutta	475	869	507	828	526	983	556	1,018	552	Not available.
Suburbs	638	...	626	...	669		Not available.	...	Not available.	...

Figures showing the natural population of the Suburbs are not available.

SUBSIDIARY TABLE II.—Number of Females per 1,000 Males at different age-periods by religions at each of the last three Censuses.

Age.	All religions.			Hindus.			Musalmans.			Christians.		
	1891	1901.	1911.	1891.	1901.	1911.	1891.	1901.	1911.	1891.	1901.	1911.
1	2	3	4	5	6	7	8	9	10	11	12	13
CALCUTTA.												
0-1	852	861	922	874	877	943	780	808	883	947	898	885
1-2	831	904	925	826	895	958	884	914	877	914	988	883
2-3	968	953	941	986	941	950	937	907	915	970	1,003	923
3-4	908	1,008	1,017	940	991	1,028	820	1,025	1,017	972	1,045	1,012
4-5	866	968	880	812	848	865	889	879	903	983	1,016	956
Total ... 0-5	*889*	*916*	*937*	*899*	*910*	*945*	*854*	*917*	*924*	*961*	*986*	*909*
5-10	890	896	901	892	885	890	850	869	879	1,092	1,177	1,031
10-15	590	599	558	587	598	557	543	537	485	930	1,048	1,056
15-20	512	511	467	520	530	487	485	419	368	981	969	936
20-25	419	383	364	408	388	366	411	254	311	789	546	653
25-30	417	341	323	424	353	335	376	291	264	636	550	571
Total ... 0-30	*560*	*530*	*504*	*558*	*537*	*514*	*523*	*476*	*439*	*869*	*811*	*803*
30-40	412	377	337	446	399	357	329	308	264	614	620	607
40-50	463	467	423	502	504	459	361	373	314	784	664	692
50-60	583	596	592	639	648	663	450	478	417	766	637	742
60 and over ..	841	863	828	940	984	927	689	660	619	967	1,018	1,107
Total 30 and over ..	*488*	*479*	*436*	*530*	*515*	*471*	*388*	*388*	*331*	*707*	*688*	*696*
Total all ages	*596*	*507*	*475*	*545*	*527*	*495*	*457*	*435*	*390*	*805*	*761*	*760*
SUBURBS.												
0-1	Not available.	882	914	Not available.	866	911	Not available.	925	910	Not available.	375	944
1-2		1,029	1,008		1,077	1,025		920	980		4,000	1,250
2-3		1,010	941		1,020	892		1,008	987		778	2,600
3-4		1,035	996		981	1,011		1,090	981		1,571	1,154
4-5		864	974		870	1,048		913	894		500	1,000
Total ... 0-5		*961*	*958*		*952*	*965*		*975*	*946*		*944*	*1,204*
5-10		903	919		841	932		990	900		1,143	1,118
10-15		626	636		616	598		633	082		1,429	1,250
15-20		703	715		629	624		784	882		1,074	2,278
20-25		597	587		535	504		716	745		1,565	772
25-30		463	471		423	416		551	588		400	667
Total ... 0-30		*670*	*679*		*622*	*613*		*752*	*780*		*993*	*1,037*
30-40		513	484		504	488		532	578		575	541
40-50		551	580		565	517		532	567		364	471
50-60		677	7 6		705	783		628	718		500	435
60 and over ...		801	878		828	937		752	797		1,150	636
Total 30 and over ..		*579*	*571*		*586*	*547*		*570*	*618*		*522*	*515*
Total all ages		*628*	*639*		*605*	*584*		*670*	*714*		*735*	*808*

SUBSIDIARY TABLE III.—Number of Females per 1,000 Males for certain selected castes.

Calcutta and Suburbs.

Caste.	Number of Females per 1,000 Males.						
	All ages.	0—5.	5—12.	12—15.	15—20.	20—40.	40 and over.
1	2	3	4	5	6	7	8
Agarwala	564	816	736	621	643	484	546
Baidya	647	862	908	864	708	424	784
Dhoba	548	822	754	657	603	423	526
Dusadh	378	589	566	373	372	315	391
Gandhabanik ...	682	1,043	986	800	965	[illegible]	620
Goala	315	584	550	662	331	227	315
Jolaha (Musalman) ...	413	778	562	276	291	418	384
Kahar	254	705	448	409	228	193	252
Khandait	31	80	68	29	22	24	37
Kurmi	220	354	390	494	222	166	205
Muchi	360	900	705	748	697	228	312
Pathan (Musalman) ...	303	551	536	325	319	234	259
Rajput or Chhatri ...	211	416	492	258	262	161	190
Sadgop ...	776	939	1,015	[illegible]	875	600	871
Saiyad (Musalman) ...	351	486	671	394	360	301	405
Subarnabanik	814	845	868	921	871	746	824
Sunri	490	986	787	557	482	386	430

SUBSIDIARY TABLE IV.—Actual number of births and deaths reported for each Sex during the decades 1891-1900 and 1901-10.

Year.	Number of births.			Number of deaths.			Excess (+) or deficit (−) of female births over male births.	Excess (+) or deficit (−) of Female deaths over Male deaths.	Excess (+) or deficit (−) of births over deaths.	Number of female births per 1,000 Male births.	Number of female deaths per 1,000 male deaths.
	Male.	Female.	Total.	Male.	Female.	Total.					
1	2	3	4	5	6	7	8	9	10	11	12
CALCUTTA.											
1891 ...	6,469	6,008	12,477	12,647	8,870	21,517	− 461	− 3,777	− 9,040	929	701
1892 ...	6,683	6,005	12,688	11,777	8,403	20,180	− 678	− 3,374	− 7,492	899	714
1893 ...	7,111	6,381	13,492	11,453	8,660	20,113	− 730	− 2,793	− 6,621	897	756
1894 ...	6,039	5,399	11,438	12,882	9,559	22,441	− 640	− 3,323	− 11,003	894	742
1895 ...	5,839	5,106	10,945	15,536	11,495	27,031	− 733	− 4,181	− 16,086	874	734
1896 ...	6,732	5,876	12,608	14,549	9,807	24,356	− 856	− 4,742	− 11,748	873	674
1897 ...	6,707	5,877	12,584	14,702	9,963	24,665	− 830	− 4,739	− 12,081	876	678
1898 ...	5,068	4,462	9,530	11,519	8,824	20,343	− 606	− 2,605	− 10,813	880	766
1899 ...	5,732	5,272	11,004	15,113	10,710	25,823	− 460	− 4,403	− 14,819	920	709
1900 ...	5,661	5,112	10,773	22,324	14,404	26,728	− 549	− 7,920	− 25,955	903	645
Total, 1891-1900 ...	***69,041***	***55,498***	***117,539***	***142,502***	***100,695***	***243,197***	***− 6,543***	***− 41,807***	***− 125,658***	***895***	***707***
1901 ...	4,798	4,331	9,129	19,358	13,098	32,456	− 467	− 6,260	− 23,327	903	677
1902 ...	6,358	5,764	12,122	18,639	12,771	31,410	− 594	− 5,868	− 19,248	907	685
1903 ...	6,894	6,288	13,182	17,391	12,374	29,765	− 606	− 5,017	− 16,583	912	712
1904 ...	7,911	7,339	15,250	15,858	11,465	27,323	− 572	− 4,393	− 12,073	928	723
1905 ...	8,392	7,245	15,637	18,820	13,361	32,181	− 1,147	− 5,459	− 16,544	863	710
1906 ...	7,861	7,222	15,083	17,462	12,831	30,293	− 639	− 4,631	− 15,210	919	735
1907 ...	8,526	7,698	16,224	18,347	13,595	31,942	− 828	− 4,752	− 15,718	903	741
1908 ...	8,840	8,203	17,043	16,255	11,434	27,689	− 637	− 4,821	− 10,646	928	703
1909 ...	10,206	9,217	19,423	16,369	12,577	28,946	− 989	− 3,792	− 9,523	903	768
1910 ...	8,914	8,192	17,106	13,353	10,375	23,728	− 722	− 2,978	− 6,622	919	777
Total, 1901-1910 ...	***78,700***	***71,499***	***150,199***	***171,852***	***123,881***	***295,733***	***− 7,201***	***− 47,971***	***− 145,534***	***909***	***721***
SUBURBS.											
1891 ...	503	480	983	1,270	953	2,223	− 23	− 317	− 1,240	954	750
1892 ...	440	408	848	620	583	1,203	− 32	− 37	− 355	927	941
1893 ...	488	483	971	515	454	969	− 5	− 61	+ 2	990	882
1894 ...	432	459	891	548	481	1,029	+ 27	− 67	− 138	1,062	878
1895 ...	409	381	790	650	556	1,206	− 28	− 94	− 416	932	855
1896 ...	452	371	823	656	456	1,112	− 81	− 200	− 289	821	695
1897 ...	508	506	1,014	543	409	952	− 2	− 134	+ 62	996	753
1898 ...	628	618	1,246	717	614	1,331	− 10	− 103	− 85	984	856
1899 ...	864	786	1,650	964	820	1,784	− 78	− 144	− 134	910	850
1900 ...	706	613	1,319	1,167	810	1,977	− 93	− 357	− 658	868	694
Total, 1891-1900 ...	***5,430***	***5,105***	***10,535***	***7,650***	***6,136***	***13,986***	***− 325***	***− 1,514***	***− 3,251***	***940***	***802***
1901 ...	658	548	1,206	926	759	1,685	− 110	− 167	− 479	833	820
1902 ...	825	711	1,536	813	684	1,497	− 114	− 129	+ 39	864	841
1903 ...	756	619	1,375	773	622	1,395	− 137	− 151	− 20	819	805
1904 ...	859	731	1,590	619	545	1,164	− 128	− 74	+ 426	851	880
1905 ...	820	728	1,548	734	564	1,298	− 92	− 170	+ 250	888	768
1906 ...	746	586	1,332	765	590	1,355	− 160	− 175	− 23	786	771
1907 ...	842	703	1,545	822	715	1,537	− 139	− 107	+ 8	835	870
1908 ...	914	756	1,670	622	518	1,140	− 158	− 104	+ 530	827	833
1909 ...	1,205	1,003	2,208	2,039	1,681	3,720	− 202	− 358	− 1,512	834	824
1910 ...	1,187	1,076	2,263	2,337	1,687	4,024	− 111	− 650	− 1,761	906	722
Total, 1901-1910 ...	***8,819***	***7,461***	***16,273***	***10,450***	***8,365***	***18,815***	***− 1,351***	***− 2,085***	***− 2,542***	***847***	***800***

SUBSIDIARY TABLE V.—NUMBER OF DEATHS OF EACH SEX AT DIFFERENT AGES.

AGE.	1905.		1906.		1907.		1908.		1909.		TOTAL.		Average number of female deaths per 1,000 male deaths.
	Male.	Female.	Male.	Female.	Male.	Female.	Male.	Female.	Male.	Female.	Male.	Female.	
CALCUTTA.													
0—1	3,720	2,239	2,794	2,347	2.535	2,219	2.436	2,169	2,737	2,469	13,222	1,1483	865
1—5	1,352	1,264	1.771	1,734	1,540	1,489	1,122	1,025	1,356	1,406	7,121	6,918	971
5—10	867	763	692	627	739	577	629	462	854	651	3,731	3,080	815
10—15	811	515	540	383	722	518	650	430	758	551	3,481	2,427	697
15—20	1,183	764	687	577	1,125	753	1,005	669	1,006	753	5,205	3,516	676
20—30 ...	3,136	1,583	2,080	1,409	2,674	1,544	2,323	1,886	2,018	1,339	12,831	7,351	573
30—40	2,758	1,345	2,558	1,324	2,703	1,528	2,809	1 553	2,199	1,306	13,087	7,056	539
40—50 ...	1,910	1,037	1,800	954	1.960	1,127	1,626	821	1,651	928	8,856	4,867	550
50—60	1,402	950	1,280	837	1.432	943	1,181	784	1,260	792	6,564	4,306	656
60 and over	2,701	2,901	2,451	2,549	2,908	2,890	2,514	2,145	2,531	2,350	13,105	12,858	981
Total ...	***18,890***	***13,361***	***17,469***	***12,831***	***18,347***	***13,595***	***16,255***	***11,434***	***16,369***	***12,577***	***87,253***	***63,807***	***731***
SUBURBS.													
0—1	143	118	126	88	139	129	107	75	426	346	941	741	787
1—5	79	65	73	67	133	87	78	81	240	217	603	517	857
5—10	55	43	47	40	46	40	36	39	102	85	286	246	860
10—15	31	23	44	27	35	27	27	20	74	56	211	152	720
15—20	41	46	40	44	55	44	30	43	91	89	257	266	1,035
20—30	95	71	110	82	100	84	81	50	287	197	673	484	719
30—40	69	54	86	50	91	71	57	36	226	187	529	398	752
40—45 ...	70	48	76	47	57	46	61	35	168	121	432	297	688
50—60	64	34	61	49	69	64	60	49	163	103	407	299	735
60 and over	87	78	102	96	97	123	85	90	272	281	648	668	1,059
Total ...	***734***	***564***	***765***	***590***	***822***	***715***	***629***	***518***	***2,039***	***1,681***	***4,989***	***4,068***	***817***

SUBSIDIARY TABLE VI.—AGE DISTRIBUTION OF 10,000 OF EACH SEX IN CALCUTTA AND SUBURBS.

AGE.	1911.		1901.		1891.		1881.	
	Male.	Female.	Male.	Female.	Male.	Female.	Male.	Female.
1	2	3	4	5	6	7	8	9
0—1	135	251	130	217				
1—2	67	126	90	158				
2-3	120	226	117	216				
3—4	118	243	115	225				
4—5	117	212	120	201				
5—10	609	1,113	876	996				
10—15	785	835	726	841				
15—20	910	911	913	929				
20—25	1,388	1,095	1,265	994				
25—30	1,454	990	1,381	937		Not available.		
30—35	1,330	975	1,209	979				
35—40	847	587	820	622				
40—45	655	730	906	826				
45—50	383	354	424	393				
50—55	414	500	476	562				
55—60	146	190	201	228				
60 and over	382	645	411	678				
Mean age	*22·1*	*27·7*	*22·7*	*28·6*				

SUBSIDIARY TABLE VII.—Age distribution of 1,000 of each Sex in certain castes.

Caste.	Males—Number per mille aged					Females—Number per mille aged				
	0—5.	5—12.	12—15.	15—40.	40 and over.	0—5.	5—12.	12—15.	15—40.	40 and over.
1	2	3	4	5	6	7	8	9	10	11
Agarwala	64	88	52	577	219	92	115	57	524	212
Baidya	88	108	64	572	168	117	151	95	433	204
Dhoba	73	99	59	548	221	110	138	72	465	215
Dosadh	57	83	52	558	253	89	119	52	479	261
Goala	41	54	43	603	259	76	93	91	481	259
Gandhabanik	82	98	58	513	249	125	141	68	436	230
Jolaha (Musalman)	58	101	103	520	218	109	137	69	482	203
Kahar	82	56	58	617	237	90	99	94	483	234
Khandait	33	35	56	634	242	91	76	53	488	292
Kurmi	50	60	51	575	264	81	106	113	455	245
Muchi	49	71	42	599	239	124	139	87	443	207
Pathan (Musalman) ...	54	77	63	578	228	97	136	68	481	218
Rajput (Chhatri)	43	56	39	622	240	85	131	47	521	216
Sadgop	71	80	56	534	259	86	104	69	451	290
Saiyad (Musalman)	77	81	58	553	231	99	142	59	454	246
Subarnabanik	101	111	74	460	254	104	119	84	436	257
Sunri	67	84	49	562	238	186	134	55	465	210

SUBSIDIARY TABLE VIII.—Proportion of Children under 10 and of Persons over 60 to those aged 15—40; also of married Females aged 15—40 per 100 Females.

	Proportion of Children, both sexes, per 100.				Proportion of Persons over 60 per 100 aged 15—40.				Number of married females aged 15—40 per 100 females of all ages.	
	Persons aged 15—40.		Married females aged 15—40.		1911.		1901.			
	1911.	1901.	1911.	1901.	Male.	Female.	Male.	Female.	1911.	1901.
Calcutta and Suburbs.	27	27	132	129	6	14	7	15	34	38

SUBSIDIARY TABLE IX.—Variation in Population at certain age periods.

	Period.	Variation per cent. in Population (Increase + Decrease —).					
		All ages.	0 — 10.	10 — 15.	15 — 40.	40 — 60.	60 and over.
Calcutta and Suburbs.	1901 — 1911	+ 9·9	+ 14·3	+ 9·2	+ 14·0	— 1·9	+ 2·7

SUBSIDIARY TABLE X.—Reported Birth and Death rates by Sex.

Year.	Number per 1,000 of total Population (Census of 1901).			
	Births.		Deaths.	
	Male.	Female.	Male.	Female.
1	2	3	4	5
CALCUTTA AND SUBURBS.				
1901	6	5	21	
1902	8	7	20	14
1903	8	7	19	14
1904	9	9	17	13
1905	10	8	21	15
1906	9	8	19	14
1907	10	9	20	15
1908	10	9	18	13
1909	12	11	19	15
1910	11	10	17	13
Average of decade	*9*	*8*	*19*	*14*

SUBSIDIARY TABLE XI.—DISTRIBUTION BY CIVIL CONDITION OF 1,000 OF EACH SEX, RELIGION AND MAIN AGE PERIOD AT EACH OF THE LAST THREE CENSUSES.

Calcutta.

RELIGION, SEX AND AGE.	UNMARRIED.			MARRIED.			WIDOWED.		
	1911.	1901.	1891.	1911.	1901.	1891.	1911.	1901.	1891.
ALL RELIGIONS.									
Males ...	*339*	*319*	*298*	*625*	*637*	*663*	*36*	*44*	*39*
0—5	995	994	994	5	6	6	0·1	0·03	0·2
5—10	978	967	976	22	31	22	0·3	2	2
10—15	889	863	845	109	132	149	2	5	6
15—20	686	614	541	308	372	447	6	14	12
20—40	186	165	148	787	804	826	27	31	26
40—60	37	44	38	886	861	879	77	95	83
60 and over ...	32	34	24	773	762	794	195	204	182
Females ...	*284*	*257*	*245*	*464*	*462*	*451*	*252*	*281*	*304*
0—5	995	992	989	4	7	10	1	1	1
5—10	949	924	933	48	70	61	3	6	6
10—15	483	447	430	498	521	536	19	32	34
15—20	101	105	102	824	808	797	75	87	101
20—40	51	36	31	727	710	676	222	254	294
40—60	27	16	14	376	374	355	597	610	631
60 and over ...	18	14	6	133	152	152	849	834	842
HINDU.									
Males ...	*335*	*312*	*290*	*627*	*642*	*666*	*38*	*46*	*44*
0—5	995	995	995	5	5	4	0·1	...	1
5—10	980	966	974	20	32	24	0·3	2	2
10—15	887	862	838	111	133	156	2	5	6
15—20	679	608	535	314	381	452	7	11	13
20—40	173	149	140	798	819	831	29	32	29
40—60	37	45	37	876	852	866	87	103	97
60 and over ...	33	33	25	752	748	770	215	219	205
Females ...	*261*	*230*	*216*	*453*	*448*	*425*	*286*	*322*	*359*
0—5	995	992	990	5	7	9	0·2	1	1
5—10	948	914	920	50	78	71	2	8	9
10—15	381	327	317	595	632	639	24	41	44
15—20	41	46	52	871	850	827	88	104	121
20—40	40	23	21	690	663	610	270	314	369
40—60	25	13	12	332	326	297	643	661	691
60 and over ...	16	14	5	110	128	117	874	858	878
MUSALMAN.									
Males ...	*312*	*295*	*277*	*659*	*665*	*693*	*29*	*40*	*30*
0—5	995	991	990	5	9	10	...	0·1	0·1
5—10	969	962	977	31	35	22	0·4	3	1
10—15	880	845	835	118	149	159	2	6	6
15—20	669	588	514	326	389	475	5	23	11
20—40	166	147	124	810	823	854	24	30	22
40—60	23	27	23	923	900	921	64	73	56
60 and over ...	15	28	14	833	801	847	152	171	139
Females ...	*288*	*263*	*260*	*523*	*522*	*535*	*189*	*210*	*205*
0—5	993	988	985	5	11	15	2	1	0·4
5—10	944	927	946	53	68	52	3	5	2
10—15	584	551	522	403	428	458	13	21	20
15—20	78	72	51	870	866	875	52	62	74
20—40	20	21	16	855	842	842	125	137	142
40—60	8	9	6	490	480	494	502	511	500
60 and over ...	8	6	3	181	190	219	811	804	778
CHRISTIAN.									
Males ...	*604*	*600*	*608*	*360*	*351*	*359*	*36*	*49*	*33*
0—5	999	1,000	1,000	1	...	...	...	...	...
5—10	995	1,000	999	5	...	...	...	...	1
10—15	983	1,000	988	16	...	16	1	...	1
15—20	960	918	823	39	85	172	1	2	5
20—40	553	558	525	428	416	458	20	26	17
40—60	155	154	191	752	702	715	93	144	94
60 and over ...	131	100	104	605	614	655	264	286	241
Females ...	*505*	*503*	*511*	*363*	*350*	*350*	*139*	*147*	*139*
0—5	998	1,000	1,000	2	...	...	..	...	...
5—10	995	1,000	997	3	...	2	2	...	1
10—15	970	970	959	28	27	37	2	3	4
15—20	723	716	671	261	370	295	16	14	84
20—40	269	247	242	645	633	656	86	120	102
40—60	132	89	93	496	496	455	372	415	452
60 and over ...	108	70	56	195	263	252	597	667	692

SUBSIDIARY TABLE XI.—Distribution by Civil Condition of 1,000 of each Sex, Religion and Main Age Period at each of the last two Censuses.

Suburbs.

Religion, Sex and Age.	Unmarried. 1911.	Unmarried. 1901.	Married. 1911.	Married. 1901.	Widowed. 1911.	Widowed. 1901.
All Religions.						
Males.	*359*	*325*	*593*	*626*	*48*	*80*
0—5	998	999	2	1	...	...
5—10	984	974	15	25	1	1
10—15	888	887	109	198	3	5
15—20	644	608	344	392	12	10
20—40	178	143	789	821	33	36
40—60	34	36	865	858	101	106
60 and over ...	25	25	738	782	237	193
Females.	*257*	*230*	*493*	*483*	*250*	*287*
0—5	995	998	5	2	...	...
5—10	924	902	74	91	2	7
10—15	371	352	604	606	25	42
15—20	38	41	885	861	77	98
20—40	15	14	770	719	215	267
40—60	12	7	371	371	617	622
60 and over ...	5	4	117	151	878	845
Hindu.						
Males.	*346*	*317*	*601*	*626*	*53*	*57*
0—5	998	999	2	1	...	...
5—10	987	976	13	23	2	1
10—15	895	897	103	96	2	7
15—20	666	618	324	378	10	11
20—40	187	152	776	808	37	40
40—60	40	45	842	828	118	127
60 and over ...	30	27	697	766	273	207
Females.	*225*	*201*	*458*	*456*	*317*	*343*
0—5	996	998	4	2	...	...
5—10	916	870	81	119	3	11
10—15	280	248	682	696	38	56
15—20	24	33	864	847	112	120
20—40	10	10	695	650	295	340
40—60	5	6	292	318	703	676
60 and over ...	4	4	84	148	912	854
Musalman.						
Males.	*378*	*335*	*582*	*630*	*40*	*35*
0—5	997	999	3	1	...	...
5—10	981	970	18	30	1	5
10—15	879	874	118	123	3	3
15—20	602	598	385	399	13	8
20—40	139	117	822	854	39	29
40—60	20	21	907	914	73	65
60 and over ...	16	19	799	811	185	170
Females.	*295*	*273*	*543*	*529*	*162*	*198*
0—5	994	998	6	2	...	...
5—10	931	942	67	56	2	2
10—15	456	473	532	503	12	25
15—20	45	40	924	896	31	64
20—40	18	17	877	834	105	149
40—60	21	7	497	475	482	518
60 and over ...	8	5	170	166	822	829
Christian.						
Males.	*605*	*568*	*367*	*391*	*28*	*41*
0—5	1,000	1,000	...	...	...	...
5—10	1,000	1,000	...	...	...	...
10—15	1,000	1,000	...	...	...	...
15—20	1,000	1,000	...	...	...	...
20—40	496	558	486	423	19	19
40—60	220	53	692	800	88	147
60 and over ...	600	...	200	1,000	200	...
Females.	*555*	*460*	*387*	*479*	*58*	*68*
0—5	1,000	1,000	...	...	...	...
5—10	1,000	1,000	...	...	...	...
10—15	982	950	18	50	...	...
15—20	659	724	317	441	24	35
20—40	190	160	756	802	54	38
40—60	214	...	548	767	238	233
60 and over ...		...	286	236	714	714

SUBSIDIARY TABLE XII.—Distribution by Main Age Periods and Civil condition of 10,000 of each Sex and Religion.

Religion and Age.	Males. Unmarried.	Males. Married.	Males. Widowed.	Females. Unmarried.	Females. Married.	Females. Widowed.
1	2	3	4	5	6	7
Calcutta.						
All religions—	*3,399*	*6,952*	*356*	*9,840*	*4,639*	*9,521*
0—10	9,860	137	3	9,715	268	17
10—15	8,895	1,066	19	4,828	4,961	191
15—40	2,629	7,133	238	611	7,462	1,927
40 and over	363	8,662	975	250	3,116	6,634
Hindus—	*3,348*	*6,269*	*383*	*9,614*	*4,529*	*9,857*
0—10	9,868	129	3	9,708	278	14
10—15	8,869	1,113	18	3,812	5 950	238
15—40	2,509	7,237	254	404	7,261	2,335
40 and over	363	8,563	1,074	230	2,749	7,021
Musalmans—	*3,119*	*6,586*	*295*	*9,881*	*5 228*	*1,891*
0—10	9,811	187	2	9,670	302	28
10—15	8,796	1,182	22	5,844	4,032	124
15—40	2,441	7,348	211	311	8,581	1,108
40 and over	210	9,059	731	77	3,980	5,943
Christians—	*6,044*	*3,599*	*357*	*5,045*	*3,033*	*1,322*
0—10	9,969	31	......	9,965	26	9
10—15	9,826	163	11	9,698	280	22
15—40	6,121	3,704	175	3,646	5,640	714
40 and over	1,512	7,259	1 229	1,358	4,205	4,437
Suburbs.						
All religions—	*3,594*	*5,929*	*477*	*9,574*	*4,931*	*9,495*
0—10	9,906	91	3	9,591	397	12
10—15	8,885	1,088	27	3,712	6,038	252
15—40	2,425	7,235	340	191	7,922	1,884
40 and over	321	8,401	1,278	102	3,027	6,871
Hindus—	*3,469*	*6,011*	*527*	*9,959*	*4,582*	*3,166*
0—10	9,923	76	1	9,557	428	15
10—15	8,949	1,026	25	2,804	6,822	374
15—40	2,565	7,100	335	127	7,271	2,602
40 and over	383	8,149	1,468	46	2,361	7,593
Musalmans—	*3,780*	*5,821*	*399*	*9,955*	*5,429*	*1,611*
0—10	9,886	109	5	9,621	369	10
10—15	8,786	1,185	29	4,558	5,318	124
15—40	2,069	7,556	355	238	8 865	897
40 and over	190	8,838	972	178	4,104	5,718
Christians—	*6,045*	*3,672*	*283*	*5,548*	*3,869*	*583*
0—10	10,000	......	......	10,000	...	......
10—15	10,000	...	...	9,818	182	......
15—40	5,280	4,545	175	2,823	6,099	473
40 and over	2,574	6,436	990	1,837	5,102	3,061

SUBSIDIARY TABLE XIII.—Proportion of the Sexes by Civil Condition at certain ages for the Main Religions.

Calcutta and Suburbs, and Religion.	Number of Females per 1,000 Males. All ages. Unmarried.	All ages. Married.	All ages. Widowed.	0—10. Unmarried.	0—10. Married.	0—10. Widowed.	10—15. Unmarried.	10—15. Married.	10—15. Widowed.	15—40. Unmarried.	15—40. Married.	15—40. Widowed.	40 and over. Unmarried.	40 and over. Married.	40 and over. Widowed.
1	2	3	4	5	6	7	8	9	10	11	12	13	14	15	16
Calcutta.															
All religions	397	352	3,366	905	1,794	6,176	303	2,560	5,659	84	377	2,920	369	198	3,649
Hindu	387	338	3,696	906	1,987	4,588	239	2,978	7,208	60	375	3,445	373	189	3,842
Musalman	360	310	2,502	887	1,459	10,750	322	1,654	7,778	87	342	1,533	117	175	3,235
Christian	834	767	2,819	966	816	..	1,042	1,821	2,000	389	995	2,658	648	451	2,878
Suburbs.															
All religions	453	526	3,307	903	4,088	4,000	266	3,528	6,000	43	591	2,990	207	231	3,487
Hindu	380	445	3,506	918	5,370	10,000	186	3,946	8,800	24	487	3,699	78	188	3,863
Musalman	558	665	2,891	897	3,113	2,000	354	3,060	2,889	76	731	1,682	610	302	3,826
Christian	741	851	1,667	1,160	...	..	1,247	..	...	391	1,077	2,000	846	385	1,500

SUBSIDIARY TABLE XIV.—Distribution of Civil condition of 1,000 of each Sex at certain Ages for selected Castes.

Calcutta and Suburbs.

Males.

Caste.	All ages. Unmarried.	All ages. Married.	All ages. Widowed.	0–5. Unmarried.	0–5. Married.	0–5. Widowed.	5–12. Unmarried.	5–12. Married.	5–12. Widowed.	12–20. Unmarried.	12–20. Married.	12–20. Widowed.	20–40. Unmarried.	20–40. Married.	20–40. Widowed.	40 and over. Unmarried.	40 and over. Married.	40 and over. Widowed.
1	2	3	4	5	6	7	8	9	10	11	12	13	14	15	16	17	18	19
Agarwala	286	664	50	1,000	...	...	937	63	...	505	487	8	119	841	40	25	841	134
Baidya	470	494	36	998	2	...	996	4	...	836	164	...	236	733	35	42	813	146
Dhoba	311	625	64	996	4	...	905	94	1	554	432	14	114	838	48	13	804	183
Dosadh	228	710	62	984	16	...	845	154	1	491	433	21	70	872	58	14	861	125
Goala	253	701	46	1,000	...	...	920	80	...	647	347	6	129	835	36	24	868	103
Gandhabanik	371	569	60	992	8	...	984	14	2	721	266	13	175	768	57	36	829	135
Jolaha (Musalman)	268	691	41	989	11	...	918	87	...	293	687	20	112	851	37	18	880	102
Kahar	214	733	53	994	6	...	937	63	...	429	563	8	104	844	52	21	872	107
Khandait	255	701	44	994	6	...	951	49	...	447	523	30	204	767	29	20	880	100
Kurmi	232	711	57	990	10	...	944	56	...	467	515	18	116	835	49	21	864	115
Muchi	214	749	37	998	2	...	947	53	...	667	333	...	55	916	29	11	900	89
Pathan (Musalman)	310	649	4	997	3	...	965	35	...	577	408	15	157	805	38	21	896	90
Rajput or Chhatri ...	300	635	65	996	4	...	943	57	...	568	408	24	212	736	63	66	818	121
Sadgop	360	576	64	998	2	...	992	8	..	747	251	2	187	756	57	37	813	150
Saiyad (Musalman)	344	610	46	1,000	..	...	976	24	...	648	349	9	158	801	41	43	845	113
Subarnabanik	421	530	49	999	1	...	982	17	1	749	241	10	161	801	38	96	772	132
Sunri	314	634	52	1,000	...	...	989	11	...	629	371	...	129	825	46	23	847	131

Females.

Caste.	All ages. Unmarried.	All ages. Married.	All ages. Widowed.	0–5. Unmarried.	0–5. Married.	0–5. Widowed.	5–12. Unmarried.	5–12. Married.	5–12. Widowed.	12–20. Unmarried.	12–20. Married.	12–20. Widowed.	20–40. Unmarried.	20–40. Married.	20–40. Widowed.	40 and over. Unmarried.	40 and over. Married.	40 and over. Widowed.
1	20	21	22	23	24	25	26	27	28	29	30	31	32	33	34	35	36	37
Agarwala	219	616	165	1,000	...	..	844	152	4	128	785	87	13	894	93	10	465	525
Baidya	296	505	199	998	2	...	853	147	..	186	774	40	16	759	225	6	384	610
Dhoba	297	510	193	995	5	...	842	150	8	180	759	61	103	738	159	5	409	586
Dosadh	215	600	185	1,000	...	...	777	223	..	176	797	27	19	843	138	6	506	488
Goala	204	517	279	998	2	...	763	234	3	211	676	113	20	671	309	19	428	553
Gandhabanik	282	474	244	997	3		867	128	5	105	841	54	30	695	286	10	332	668
Jolaha (Musalman)	284	576	146	993	7	...	823	166	11	233	715	47	57	841	102	6	544	450
Kahar	234	578	188	998	2	...	773	225	2	228	724	48	62	780	158	5	496	499
Khandait	287	453	260	1,000	...	..	923	77	...	354	542	104	102	628	270	120	410	470
Kurmi	204	577	219	1,000	...		828	172	...	130	814	56	21	763	211	10	463	527
Muchi	272	531	189	976	24	...	798	202	...	190	745	65	7	779	214	6	488	506
Pathan (Musalman)	272	565	163	996	4	...	914	83	3	191	762	47	26	821	153	21	524	455
Rajput or Chhatri ...	245	515	240	996	4	...	913	87	...	172	767	61	26	708	266	7	425	568
Sadgop	208	432	360	934	4	2	808	179	13	155	701	144	6	598	396	25	285	690
Saiyad (Musalman)	300	517	183	1,000	...	...	937	53	10	251	670	79	58	772	170	29	526	445
Subarnabanik	251	510	239	984	16	...	890	108	2	188	757	55	16	732	252	8	428	564
Sunri	263	491	239	995	5		846	154	...	79	857	64	14	745	241	6	314	680

CHAPTER VI.

NATIONALITY, RACE AND CASTE.

67. It is no exaggeration of language to describe the population of Calcutta and the Suburbs as an agglomeration of races, for no less than 397 separate nationalities, races and castes are returned. Nearly all the races and nationalities of the civilized world are represented. and the castes are drawn from all over India, the number of their representatives varying from one to over a quarter of a million.

EUROPEAN AND ALLIED RACES.

68. The aggregate of persons who come under the heading "Europeans and allied races" is 13,808, of whom 13,482 were enumerated in Calcutta and 326 in the Suburbs: all but 1,423 are British subjects. The term "allied races", it may be explained, is applied to such non-European races as Australians, Americans, Canadians, etc. Approximately two-thirds of the Europeans are English, one-eighth are Scotch and 7 per cent. are Irish. In other words, there are 9 Englishmen to every two Scotchmen, and 10 Englishmen to every Irishman Six other races have over 100 representatives as shown in the margin. The English have increased in number by nearly 1,000 since 1901, and the Scotch by almost 500. The premier race of the Empire, however, is now less strongly represented, and comes third on the list, whereas it was second in 1901: the explanation is simply that, at the time of the last census, an Irish regiment was stationed in the Fort. There has been a considerable addition to the German community, and the Portuguese are also more numerous; most of the latter are probably Goanese and not pure Portuguese.

Race.	Number.
English	9,423
Scotch	1,668
Irish	996
German ...	282
Portuguese	264
French	216
Greek	131
American	111
Australian	109

VARIATIONS SINCE 1901.

69. Since 1901 the European community of Calcutta and the Suburbs has increased by only 756 the smallness of the growth being due to the reduction in the number of Europeans enumerated in the Port. In Calcutta proper, *i.e.*, the area within municipal limits, there is an increase of 2,056 or 23 per cent., bringing up the aggregate to 10,978; males have increased by 1,568 or 31·7 per cent., and females by 488 or 12·3 per cent. In five adjacent wards to the north and north-east, viz., Barabazar, Kalutola, Muchipara, Bowbazar and Entally, there is a loss of 384, but in the remainder of Calcutta there is a gain of 2,440 or 35 per cent. The five wards where the better class of Europeans reside. viz., Collinga, Park Street, Victoria Terrace (or Baman Bustee), Ballygunge-Tollygunge and Alipore, now contain 3,910 Europeans, or nearly two-fifths of the total number enumerated in the municipal area, the net increment since 1901 being no less than 1,822 or 87 per cent. The figures for Park Street are remarkable. Here the number of Europeans has increased five-fold, rising from 230 to 1,158: males are more numerous by 541 and females by 384.

70. While there has been such a large addition in Calcutta proper, there has been a remarkable diminution in the number enumerated in the Port (viz., from 2,374 to 1,047), for which I am unable to account. Though the Port population includes passengers on steamers, as well as ships' officers, sailors, firemen, boatmen, etc., it is difficult to understand how the number of Europeans could have reached 2,374 in 1901 One hypothesis that might be put forward is that a large number of homeward-bound passengers were enumerated on steamers leaving Calcutta—as is well known, the outward bound steamers that arrive in Calcutta early in March, when the census is held, carry very few passengers, and they may therefore be left out of account There is, however, no record of any crowded passenger steamers being enumerated in 1901, and as a matter of fact, the steamers are not crowded so early in the year as the 1st March when the census took place. In any case, too, the supposition seems to

be precluded by the small number of European women recorded, viz., 85, or only 58 more than at this census. Another point which calls for notice is that the percentage of Europeans to the total population of the Port is, as shown in the margin, less than half what it was 10 years ago, but is a little below that registered in 1891.* It is only natural that it should fall short of what it was 20 years ago, for large sailing ships with European crews very rarely come up the Hooghly, and it is a matter of common knowledge that European seamen have been largely superseded by lascars on steamers engaged in the eastern trade. This, however, cannot altogether account for the reduction in the number of Europeans during the last 10 years, for even in 1901 sailing vessels had, to a great extent, given place to steamers and lascars were being employed instead of European sailors. It is, therefore, all the more surprising that at the last census Europeans should have constituted 8 per cent. of the population of the Port, *i.e.*, approximately one out of every 12 persons enumerated on vessels of all kinds, including barges, flats, country boats, etc. It is, moreover, noticeable that in 1901 the daily average European population of the Port (as calculated from the weekly shipping list and the inspection figures of all incoming vessels) was only 1,150, and that the average of the five years ending in 1901 was 1,154. It may be added that the figure now returned (1,047) very closely corresponds to that obtained at an enumeration held by the Port Health Officer on an average day in 1910, viz., 1,056.

Year.	Number of Europeans.	Percentage to total population.
1891	1,263	4·7
1901	2,374	7·9
1911	1,047	3·9

71. The Anglo-Indians (a name prescribed by the Government of India for the community of mixed descent previously known as Eurasians) number 14,469, of whom all but 292 were enumerated in Calcutta. Since 1901 there has been a falling off of 191 in their numbers, which is due to the loss of 305 in Calcutta, for in the Suburbs there has been a gain of 114. This may point to a small movement to the suburban area and to a larger movement in search of employment outside Calcutta: but it seems more probable that the decrease is due to a number of Anglo-Indians declaring themselves to be Europeans. That they frequently describe themselves as Europeans is a familiar fact, which is confirmed by special inquiries regarding the correctness of the entries of race made by Anglo-Indians in other towns where they are specially numerous. The result of these inquiries was to show that three-tenths of the Anglo-Indians returned themselves as Europeans, and that even in railway settlements where the record of race was more accurate, every one in ten did so. The marginal statement shows the wards in which the Anglo-Indian community has the greatest strength.

ANGLO-INDIANS.

Ward.	Number.	Percentage to total number.
Bowbazar ...	2,987	21
Taltola	1,760	12½
Kalutola	1,530	11
Entally	1,333	9½
Fenwick Bazar ...	1,271	9
Paddapukur ...	1,190	8½

72. The number of persons returned as Armenians is 832, of which Calcutta alone accounts for 815. The community is practically stationary, having added only 40 to its numbers during the last ten years. Five-eighths were returned as members of the Armenian Church, and less than three-eighths as speaking Armenian; practically all the remainder use English habitually. A considerable number are new arrivals from Persia, and in particular from Julfa. When they land they are ignorant of English, but they soon learn the language and rapidly assimilate European ways. Calcutta being regarded as a good place at which to give Armenian boys a start in life, and the knowledge of English a valuable commercial asset, they are frequently sent there from Persia to receive an English education. Half the number of Armenian males in Calcutta were born in Persia, but the number of females hailing from that country was insignificant; over one-fourth of those born in Persia were under 15 years of age.

ARMENIANS.

* The census of the Port was defective in 1891 and less Europeans were enumerated than in 1881, *cf.* paragraph 56, page 19 of the Report of 1891), but this does not affect the proportional figures.

73. There are altogether 1,920 Jews in Calcutta and the Suburbs, or 31 more than there were 10 years ago. They consist of two main classes, viz., domiciled Jews and Asiatic immigrants. A certain number of the former are European Jews, some of whom are Sephardim, *i.e.*, descendants of the Spanish Jews that were driven out of Spain by the Inquisition. The latter are mostly new-comers from Arabia or Asiatic Turkey, who, when they arrive, are ignorant of English. Nearly one-third returned their language as English, and practically all the rest spoke either Hebrew or Arabic. Three-fifths were born in Calcutta and one-sixth in Arabia.

JEWS.

74. While the Armenians and the Jews show no tendency to increase, the Chinese colony is growing rapidly not so much by natural reproduction as by the influx of new immigrants from China. There are now 2,560 of these Orientals, and they are more numerous by 921 than they were 10 years ago.

CHINESE.

75. The Brahmans are by far the most numerous of the Hindu castes in Calcutta and the Suburbs, having a strength of 107,141 or nearly one-sixth of the total number of Hindus. Next, in order, come the Kayasths (86,644) and the Kaibarttas (43,970); three-fourths of the latter are Chasi Kaibarttas or Mahishyas. The Chamars have 33,808, the Goalas 31,480, the Subarnabaniks 28,780, the Kahars 24,006, the Tantis 21,751 and the Telis and Tilis 20,646 representatives. No other Hindu caste exceeds 20,000. Of the nine castes mentioned, only the Kaibarttas and Subarnabaniks are indigenous to Bengal; the others include immigrants from widely distant parts of India. One remarkable feature of the returns is the paucity of the Namasudras and Rajbansis, two of the chief castes in Bengal. The Namasudras of the Province aggregate nearly 2 millions, but contribute only 2,084 to the population of Calcutta and the Suburbs, while the Rajbansis' share is 604, though they number 1,700,000. Equally noticeable is the fact that, though the Pods are found to the number of 470,000 in the 24-Parganas and Khulna, less than 3,000 have come to the metropolis.

INDIAN CASTES.

Among the Musalmans the Sheikhs predominate, numbering 257,170 or nearly nine-tenths of the total number that have the faith of Islam. This designation is now frequently used as a generic term by the lower Musalman groups who aspire to a more respectable status; a common proverb is "Last year I was Jolaha, this year I am a Sheikh." As most of the Musalmans are immigrants, it is easier for them to assume the more pleasing name of Sheikh than in their own villages where their real origin is known. It is this tendency which largely accounts for the paucity of Jolahas, of whom only 8,864 were returned. The number of the latter is less than half that of the Pathans (21,025), a large proportion of whom are immigrants from up-country.

76. Statistics showing the variations in the numbers of the principal castes since 1901 will be found in the subsidiary table at the end of this chapter. The variations are often extraordinary, and it must be explained that the figures are affected by three factors. In the first place, the census of 1901 was more complete and accurate than its predecessors, the result being an abnormal increase of many castes, which does not represent real growth. Secondly, variations may be due to difference of procedure in enumeration and compilation. For example, Khatri is a name which i is exceedingly difficult to distinguish from Chhatri (*i.e.*, Rajput) as spelt in the vernacular, so that the number of Khatris in the caste table is, to some extent, a matter of chance. There are, moreover, 65 more Hindu castes recorded than in 1901, the addition being due to the care taken to distinguish and obtain a record of small foreign castes. Many of these must have been merged in other groups during compilation in 1901. Lastly, immigration often produces surprising results. For example, the Oriya caste of Khandaits has nearly doubled its numbers in the last 10 years, the Bhuiyas have actually done so, and the foreign trading castes, known as Mahesri and Agarwala, have each grown by about 150 per cent. Perhaps the

VARIATIONS SINCE 1901.

most remarkable figure is that recorded for the Jolahas, who have increased over fifty-fold, their number rising from 166 to 8,864. It is incredible that this large Musalman group, from which so many of the mill hands are drawn, should have constituted such a minute fraction of the population in 1901. The explanation is that in that year they must have returned themselves as Sheikhs. The separate record of these Jolahas is mainly responsible for the decrease of nearly 5,000 in the number returned as Sheikhs. Another noticeable feature is the large increase of Chasi Kaibarttas or Mahishyas, a progressive section of the Kaibarttas, who claim a status superior to that of other Kaibartta groups. The total number of Kaibarttas of all kinds is very much the same as in 1901, but nearly 29,000 more have described themselves as Chasi Kaibarttas or Mahishyas; those who are differentiated as Julia Kaibarttas have increased by over 3,500; and there is a falling off of 34,000 in the number of those who are content to call themselves simply Kaibarttas without specifying the Kaibartta group to which they belong. These figures sufficiently show how rapidly the fission of this caste into distinct sections is proceeding.

	1911.	1901.
Kaibartta Chasi	31,961	3,359
" Julia	4,218	584
" Unspecified ..	7,791	41,775
Total ...	43,970	45,718

SUBSIDIARY TABLE I.—VARIATIONS IN THE PRINCIPAL CASTES, TRIBES, AND RACES, SINCE 1891.

Caste, Tribe or Race.	Calcutta. Total number. 1911.	1901.	1891.	Percentage of variation, increase (+), decrease (−). 1901-1911.	1891-1901.	Suburbs. Total number. 1911.	1901.	Percentage of variation, increase (+), decrease (−) 1901-1911.
1	2	3	4	5	6	1	2	3
HINDU, BRAHMO, JAIN, ETC.								
Agarwala	10,944	4,400	1,371	+ 148·7	· 220·9	...	...	...
Bagdi	4,867	7,182	7,007	− 32·2	+ 2·5	4,220	3,894	+ 8·4
Baidya	8,548	7,100	4,495	+ 20·4	+ 58·0	...	...	...
Baishnab and Bairagi	12,802	14,270	17,053	− 10·3	16·3	4,204	3,878	+ 8·5
Bais Baniya	3,834	2,529	...	+ 51·6	...	...	..	...
Barui and Barui	1,877	1,774	1,336	+ 5·8	+ 32·8	...	..	...
Bhar	...	...	...	..	...	465	231	+ 101·3
Bhuiya	2,127	1,022	548	+ 108·1	+ 86·5	694	...	...
Brahman	99,371	82,710	62,375	+ 20·1	+ 32·6	7,540	6,071	+ 29·1
Chamar	27,073	24,586	24,811	+ 10·1	− [illegible]	6,735	5,024	+ 34·1
Dhoba	9,217	9,826	7,879	− 6·2	+ 24·7	1,764	1,364	[illegible] 29·3
Dom	5,490	9,625	3,377	− 43·0	+ 185·0	534	921	− 42·0
Dosadh	8,803	7,787	6,582	+ 13·0	+ 19·2	1,913	953	+ 100·7
Gandhabanik	7,187	9,468	14,223	− 24·1	33·4	452	602	− 24·9
Goala	26,561	22,947	20,258	+ 15·7	+ 13·3	4,924	3,339	+ 47·5
Hari	2,939	1,581	895	+ 89·7	+ 76·[illegible]	353	87	+ 305·7
Jogi and Jugi	2,480	2,923	2,710	− 16·9	+ 7·9	465	658	− 29·3
Kahar	22,097	19,253	14,441	+ 14·8	+ 33·3	1,921	1,028	+ 86·9
Kaibartta (Total)	33,459	34,117	28,325	− 1·9	+ 20·4	10,511	7,660	+ 37·2
„ Chasi (Mahisya)	23,921	2,123	...	+ 1,026·8	...	8,040	1,236	+ 550·5
„ Jalia	3,476	476	3,824	+ 630·3	− 87·6	742	108	+ 587·0
„ unspecified	6,062	31,518	24,501	− 80·8	+ 28·6	1,729	6,316	− 72·6
Kalu	3,764	4,314	4,064	− 12·7	+ 6·2	414	407	+ 1·7
Kalwar	3,724	9,362	2,448	− 60·2	+ 282·4	438	893	− 51·0
Kamar (Karmakar)	7,285	7,108	1,423	+ 2·5	+ 399·8	857	484	+ 77·1
Kandu	1,898	1,870	993	+ 1·5	+ 87·9	557	297	+ 87·5
Kansari	4,449	3,913	3,431	+ 13·7	+ 14·0	..	...	...
Kaora	4,177	3,302	4,529	+ 26·5	− 27·1	354	403	− 12·2
Kayasth	79,495	67,287	59,023	+ 18·1	+ 14·0	7,400	4,621	+ 60·1
Khandait	9,786	5,835	1,685	+ 67·7	+ 246·3	1,624	472	+ 244·1
Khatri	3,818	5,260	3,713	− 27·4	+ 41·7	...	..	...
Koiri	3,905	3,552	2,093	+ 9·9	+ 69·7	1,317	835	+ 57·7
Kumhar	2,403	2,127	6,650	+ 13·0	− 68·0	1,027	312	+ 229·2
Kurmi	8,397	6,320	4,865	+ 32·9	+ 29·9	1,034	823	+ 25·6
Maheshri	2,605	1,037	98	+ 151·2	+ 958·2		...	...
Mallah	2,766	3,802	...	− 27·2	..	...	...	...
Mayra	5,948	6,773	5,386	− 12·2	+ 25·8	696	573	+ 21·5
Mehtar	5,600	1,587	9,841	+ 252·9	− 83·9	809	179	+ [illegible]
Muchi	10,516	8,477	...	+ 24·1	...	2,187	948	+ 130·7
Namasudra	...	...	...	...	...	943	409	+ [illegible]
Napit	11,123	12,162	9,018	− 8·5	+ 34·9	1,510	1,303	+ 15·9
Nuniya	...	...	...	...	...	362	190	+ 90·5
Oswal	2,907	1,964	...	+ 48·0	...	...	...	...
Pasi	...	...	...	...	...	962	592	+ 62·5
Pod	...	...	...	...	...	924	303	+ 205·0
Rajput (Chhatri)	12,979	8,415	6,855	+ 54·2	+ 22·9	1,841	1,006	+ 83·0
Sadgop	10,833	11,758	10,039	7·8	+ 17·1	3,089	1,896	+ 62·9
Sonar	4,385	4,194	3,030	+ 4·6	+ 38·4	480	497	− 3·4
Subarnabanik	28,210	25,190	19,635	+ 12·0	+ 28·3	575	1,336	− 57·0
Sunri	4,140	} 7,024	5,456	− 10·2	+ 28·7	{ 708	} 586	+ 60·07
Shaha	3,169					230		
Sutradhar	5,518	5,656	5,212	− 2·4	+ 8·5	945	535	+ 76·6
Tambuli	2,906	4,937	2,947	− 41·1	± 67·5	...	..	...
Tanti and Tatwa	19,427	20,692	16,295	− 6·1	+ 27·0	2,327	1,790	+ 30·0
Teli and Tili	18,469	14,581	12,877	+ 24·5	+ 15·2	2,180	1,553	+ 40·4
Tiyar	...	...	...	...	...	959	452	+ 112·2
MUSALMAN.								
Jolaha	7,145	166	...	+ 4,204·2	...	1,719		...
Moghal	...	...	...	...	...	380	496	− 23·4
Pathan	17,160	12,555	12,453	+ 36·7	+ ·8	3,865	1,976	+ 95·6
Saiyad	6,175	6,798	4,022	− 9·2	+ 69·0	1,079	788	+ 36·9
Sheikh	207,275	228,741	185,632	− 9·4	+ 23·2	49,895	33,346	+ 49·6
CHRISTIAN.								
Anglo Indian	14,177	14,482	9,818	− 2·1	+ 47·5	...	...	...
English	9,215	8,330	...	+ 10·6	...	...	...	...

Only those castes, tribes or races are shown which contribute 2 per mille to the population of either Calcutta or the Suburbs

SUBSIDIARY TABLE II.—Variation in the number of Europeans and allied races since 1901.

	1911. Total.	1911. Male.	1911. Female.	1901. Total.	1901. Male.	1901. Female.	Total variation—Increase (+) Decrease (−) Total.	Male.	Female.
CALCUTTA WITH SUBURBS ...	*13,808*	*9,056*	*4,752*	*13,052*	*8,688*	*4,364*	*+ 756*	*+ 368*	*+ 388*
CALCUTTA	*13,482*	*8,834*	*4,648*	*12,794*	*8,526*	*4,268*	*+ 688*	*+ 308*	*+ 380*
CALCUTTA (Municipal Area) ...	*10,978*	*6,519*	*4,459*	*8,922*	*4,951*	*3,971*	*+ 2,056*	*+ 1,568*	*+ 488*
Ward No. 1, Shampukur	......	......	......	4	4	......	− 4	− 4	......
" " 2, Kumartoli	8	3	5	5	5	......	+ 3	− 2	+ 5
" " 3, Bartala	7	4	3	4	2	1	+ 3	+ 1	+ 2
" " 4, Sukea Street	62	45	17	84	59	25	− 22	− 14	− 8
" " 5, Jorabagan	32	18	14	19	15	4	+ 13	+ 3	+ 10
" " 6, Jorasanko	3	......	3	6	2	4	− 3	− 2	− 1
" " 7, Barabazar	165	136	29	266	212	54	− 101	− 76	− 25
" " 8, Kalutola	209	126	83	298	172	126	− 89	− 46	− 43
" " 9, Muchipara	266	162	104	348	166	182	− 82	− 4	− 78
" " 10, Bowbazar	703	432	271	847	430	417	− 144	+ 2	− 146
" " 11, Paddapukur	450	249	201	403	221	182	+ 47	+ 28	+ 19
" " 12, Waterloo Street ...	1,107	762	345	912	616	296	+ 195	+ 146	+ 49
" " 13, Fenwick Bazar ...	1,274	735	539	1,154	589	565	+ 120	+ 146	− 26
" " 14, Taltola	663	349	314	658	308	350	+ 5	+ 41	− 36
" " 15, Collinga	1,193	662	531	830	412	418	+ 363	+ 250	+ 113
" " 16, Park Street	1,158	702	456	230	158	72	+ 928	+ 544	+ 384
" " 17, Baman Bustee (Victoria Terrace).	812	517	295	567	359	208	+ 285	+ 158	+ 87
" " 18, Hastings	319	187	132	261	129	132	+ 58	+ 58	......
" " 19, Entally	313	158	155	451	194	257	− 138	− 36	− 102
" " 20, Beniapukur	179	85	94	133	63	70	+ 46	+ 22	+ 24
" " 21, Ballygunge-Tollygunge	456	279	177	298	150	148	+ 158	+ 129	+ 29
" " 22, Bhawanipore	678	407	271	402	267	135	+ 276	+ 140	+ 136
" " 23, Alipore	291	168	123	163	85	78	+ 128	+ 83	+ 45
" " 24, Ekbalpore	326	157	169	322	171	151	+ 4	− 14	+ 18
" " 25, Watganj	304	176	128	257	161	96	+ 47	+ 15	+ 32
Fort William and Maidan ...	*1,457*	*1,295*	*162*	*1,498*	*1,286*	*212*	*− 41*	*+ 9*	*− 50*
PORT	*1,047*	*1,020*	*27*	*2,374*	*2,289*	*85*	*− 1,327*	*− 1,269*	*− 58*
CANALS	......	......	......	......	......	......	......	......	......
Suburbs	*326*	*222*	*104*	*258*	*162*	*96*	*+ 68*	*+ 60*	*+ 8*
Cossipur-Chitpur	188	119	69	145	86	59	+ 43	+ 33	+ 10
Manicktollah	28	19	9	11	5	6	+ 17	+ 14	+ 3
Garden Reach	110	84	26	102	71	31	+ 8	+ 13	− 5

Armenians are excluded.

SUBSIDIARY TABLE III.—Variation in the number of Anglo-Indians since 1901 and their Percentage to the total number in each Ward of Calcutta.

	1911. Total.	1911. Male.	1911. Female.	1901. Total.	1901. Male.	1901. Female.	Total variation—Increase (+), Decrease (—). Total	Male.	Female.	Percentage in 1911 to total number.
CALCUTTA WITH SUBURBS.	*14,469*	*7,064*	*7,405*	*14,660*	*7,206*	*7,454*	*− 191*	*− 142*	*− 49*	
CALCUTTA	*14,177*	*6,920*	*7,257*	*14,482*	*7,115*	*7,367*	*− 305*	*− 195*	*− 110*	
CALCUTTA (Municipal Area).	*14,050*	*6,830*	*7,220*	*14,351*	*7,003*	*7,348*	*− 301*	*− 173*	*− 128*	
Ward 1, Shampukur ...	2	2	......	7	1	6	− 5	+ 1	− 6	0·01
" 2, Kumartoli ...	8	2	6	......	......	......	+ 8	+ 2	+ 6	0·06
" 3, Bartala ...	11	5	6	4	2	2	+ 7	+ 3	+ 4	0·03
" 4, Sukea Street ...	125	98	27	121	97	24	+ 4	+ 1	+ 3	0·9
" 5, Jorabagan ...	16	6	10	38	20	18	− 22	− 14	− 8	0·1
" 6, Jorasanko ...	......	......	......	......	......	......	......	......	......	......
" 7, Barabazar ...	248	236	12	278	246	28	− 25	− 9	− 16	1·8
" 8, Kalutola ...	1,530	740	790	1,970	995	975	− 440	− 255	− 185	10·9
" 9, Muchipara ...	784	384	350	541	296	245	+ 193	+ 88	+ 105	5·2
" 10, Bowbazar ...	2,987	1,473	1,514	3,456	1,713	1,743	− 469	− 240	− 229	21·2
" 11, Paddapukur ...	1,190	553	637	1,197	573	624	− 7	− 20	+ 13	8·5
" 12, Waterloo Street	201	89	112	240	120	121	− 39	− 31	− 8	1·4
" 13, Fenwick Bazar	1,271	594	677	1,325	600	725	− 54	− 6	− 48	9·04
" 14, Taltola	1,760	918	842	1,645	820	825	+ 115	+ 98	+ 17	12·5
" 15, Collinga ...	904	449	455	589	322	267	+ 315	+ 127	+ 188	6·4
" 16, Park Street ...	100	36	64	550	238	312	− 450	− 202	− 248	0·7
" 17, Baman Bustee (Victoria Terrace).	174	93	81	119	41	78	+ 55	+ 52	+ 3	1·2
" 18, Hastings ...	106	44	62	92	50	42	+ 14	− 6	+ 20	0·75
" 19, Entally	1,333	477	856	1,107	372	735	+ 226	+ 105	+ 121	9·5
" 20, Beniapukur ...	380	174	206	261	121	140	+ 119	+ 53	+ 66	2·7
" 21, Ballygunge-Tollygunge.	84	40	44	85	43	42	− 1	− 3	+ 2	0·6
" 22, Bhawanipore ...	243	116	127	192	84	108	+ 51	+ 32	+ 19	1·7
" 23, Alipore	37	9	28	66	28	38	− 29	− 19	− 10	0·26
" 24, Ekbalpore ...	368	173	193	258	118	140	+ 110	+ 57	+ 53	2·8
" 25, Watganj ...	240	119	121	217	106	111	+ 23	+ 13	+ 10	1·7
Fort William and Maidan.	*49*	*21*	*28*	*26*	*20*	*6*	*+ 23*	*+ 1*	*+ 22*	
PORT	*78*	*69*	*9*	*105*	*92*	*13*	*− 27*	*− 23*	*− 4*	
CANALS	......	......	......	......	......	......	......	......	......	
Suburbs	*292*	*144*	*148*	*178*	*91*	*87*	*+ 114*	*+ 53*	*+ 61*	
Cossipur-Chitpur ...	240	111	129	127	67	60	+ 113	+ 44	+ 69	
Manicktollah	30	20	10	23	9	14	+ 7	+ 11	− 4	
Garden Reach	22	13	9	28	15	13	− 6	− 2	− 4	

CHAPTER VII.

LANGUAGE.

General distribution.

77. Calcutta is a polyglot city, its inhabitants speaking 51 different languages. Altogether 28 different Indian tongues appear in the returns, the number of persons speaking them being a little over a million. Nine other Asiatic and African languages are returned for 5,076 persons, and 14 European languages for 9,366 persons.

Indian languages.

78. Bengali is the language of 512,579 persons or half the population, Hindi of 365,339 or one-third, and Urdu of 70,558, or nearly 7 per cent. Both Hindi and Urdu, it must be explained, have a far wider connotation than that given them in the Linguistic Survey and should perhaps be grouped together, as in many cases there is little or no difference between them. Hindi includes not only Hindi proper but also Bihari, and, in fact, represents the latter language in the majority of cases. Urdu is used in a still looser sense, for it not only refers to true Urdu, but is also a designation applied to their language by Musalman immigrants, whether they speak Hindi or Bihari. As shown in the map printed in this paragraph, the home of Bengali is the north-east of Calcutta, where it is spoken by two-thirds or more of the inhabitants of Shampukur, Kumartoli, Bartala, Sukea Street, Muchipara and Paddapukur. The only other ward in which the same proportion is reached is Bhawanipore to the south, which has a dense Bengali population. It is also spoken by one-half to two-thirds of the people in three of the southern wards, viz., Ballygunge-Tollygunge, Alipore and Ekbalpore, as well as in Jorasanko to the north, and in Garden Reach and Manicktollah.

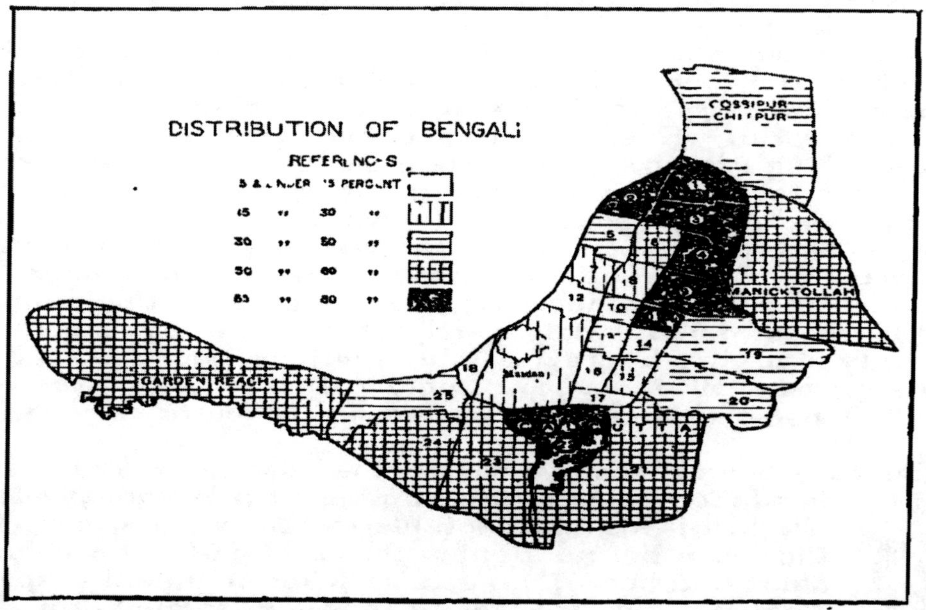

79. In Cossipur-Chitpur, in fourteen of the 25 wards of Calcutta, and in the Port, Hindi and Urdu* are more generally spoken than Bengali. Three-fourths of the people speak Hindi and Urdu in Hastings, and half to two thirds in Barabazar, Jorabagan, Kalutola, Collinga, Park Street, Entally, Beniapukur and Watganj, as well as in Cossipur-Chitpur. After Bengali, Hindi and Urdu, the most widely spoken languages are Oriya, which is returned for 41,153 persons,

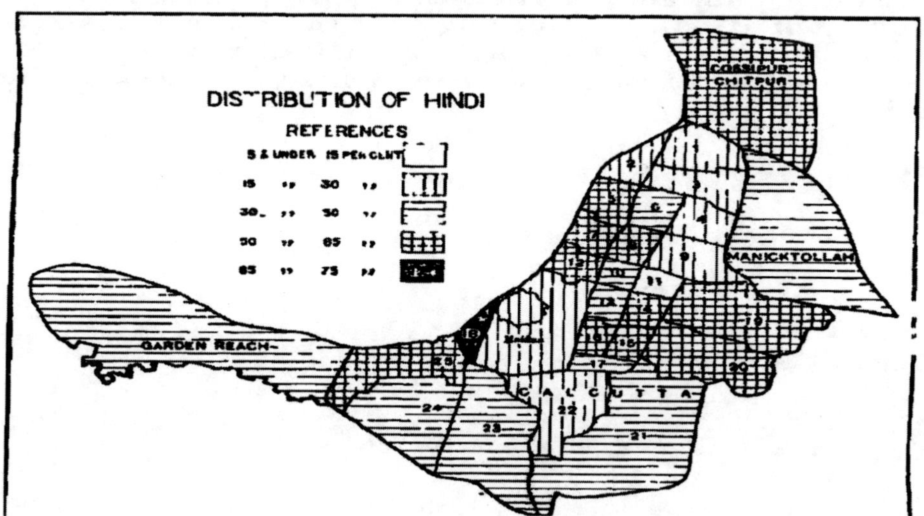

* In the the second map on this page Hindi includes Urdu.

Marwari (8,998), Gujarati (2,802), Panjabi (1,74?), Tamil (1,701) and Telugu (1,469). The remaining 19 languages are distributed between 2,5?3 persons.

OTHER LANGUAGES.

80. Of non-Indian languages English is *facile princeps*, being the mother-tongue of 28,430 persons. It is the language of nearly one-third of the people in Baman Bustee (Victoria Terrace), of a fourth in Park Street, of one fifth in Waterloo Street and Collinga, and of a little over one-seventh in Bow Bazar. Chinese has 2,611 speakers, but no other language has 1,000 representatives. Of the minor languages the most important are Persian (791) and Arabic (656), the latter being mainly spoken by immigrant Jews.

VARIATIONS SINCE 1901

81. At this census revised instructions were issued regarding the entry of language in the schedules. In 1901 it was laid down that the language to be entered was that ordinarily spoken by each person, but this led to some curious results, persons returning not their native language but that which they commonly used in intercourse with the outside world. Even persons speaking Maltese, Norwegian and Roumanian declared English to be their language. To prevent such anomalies, it was laid down at this census that the language to be returned was that which each person ordinarily spoke in his own home. This change in the instructions has led to greater accuracy in the returns. It was realized that the mother tongue was to be returned, and not that which an immigrant might use in his new environment. The increase, for example, in the number of Marwari speakers from 115 to 8,998 is only partly explicable by increased immigration, and is mainly due to the revised instructions: the number of Marwari speakers registered in 1901 was, in fact, palpably below the real number, for nearly 15,000 persons were enumerated in Calcutta who were born in Rajputana.

82. The small decrease which, as shown in the marginal statement, has taken place in the number of persons speaking English is also attributable to the same cause, for there can be no doubt that in 1901 a considerable number of persons who commonly spoke English, but to whom it was a foreign tongue, returned that and not their native language.

Language.	1911.	1901.
Bengali ...	512,579	494,420
Hindi ...	365,339	353,786
Urdu ...	7[illegible],558	27,627
Oriya .	4[illegible],153	33,498
English ...	28,430	28,979

It cannot, however, be said that the change in the instructions can have affected the returns for Bengali, the number of persons speaking which has risen by only 18,159 or less than 4 per cent. Those speaking Hindi and Urdu, on the other hand, have increased by 54,000 or 14 per cent. The figures for Urdu show what at first sight appears an abnormal growth in its popularity, for the number returning it as their mother-tongue has been more than doubled. This is due to the attitude taken up by a large number of Musalmans with regard to their language. They insisted that they spoke Urdu and were strongly averse to the entry of Hindi, considering that the former meant the language of Musalmans and the latter the language of Hindus, though as a matter of fact, in a large number of cases, neither community speaks either Hindi or Urdu, but Bihari.

SUBSIDIARY TABLE I.

NAME OF WARD.	Ward No.	NUMBER PER 10,000 OF POPULATION SPEAKING—		
		Bengali.	Hindi and Urdu.	English.
1	2	3	4	5
CALCUTTA ...	...	***4,904***	***4,106***	***311***
Shampukur ...	I	7,217	2,474	3
Kumartoli ...	II	7,753	1,881	2
Bartola ...	III	6,743	2,910	3
Sukea Street ...	IV	6,624	2,921	46
Jorabagan ...	V	3,433	5,396	9
Jorasanko ...	VI	5,623	3.523	1
Barabazar ...	VII	1 908	6,510	146
Kalutola ...	VIII	2,834	5,880	173
Muchipara ...	IX	6,510	2,996	167
Bow Bazar ...	X	3,020	3,818	1,510
Paddapukur ...	XI	6,714	1,335	556
Waterloo Street ...	XII	559	5,632	2,118
Fenwick Bazar ...	XIII	3,543	4,509	886
Taltola ...	XIV	3,753	5,172	815
Collinga ...	XV	1,762	5,574	1,995
Park Street ...	XVI	690	5,476	2,454
Victoria Terrace (Baman Bustee) ...	XVII	538	3,623	3,226
Hastings ...	XVIII	934	7,456	805
Entally ...	XIX	4,209	5,075	373
Beniapukur ...	XX	3,306	6,252	196
Ballygunge-Tollygunge ...	XXI	5,006	4,360	146
Bhawanipore ...	XXII	6,919	2,666	179
Alipore ...	XXIII	5,897	3,197	166
Ekbalpore ...	XXIV	5,097	4,136	325
Watganj ...	XXV	3,483	5,786	125
Fort William and Maidan ...	...	3,748	2,652	3,448
Port ...	...	3,843	5,074	376
Canals ...	...	5,816	4,168	...
SUBURBS	...	***4,966***	***4,615***	***41***
Cossipur-Chitpur ...	...	4,503	5,059	86
Manicktollah ...	...	5,174	4,398	10
Garden Reach ...	...	5,210	4,401	28
GRAND TOTAL ...	...	4,913	4,177	273

CHAPTER VIII.

EDUCATION.

Introductory.

83. At each of the last three censuses different instructions have been given regarding the entries in the schedules relating to education. In 1891 the same classification was adopted as in 1881, the population being divided into three classes, viz., "Learning", "Literate", and "Illiterate". Those who were under instruction, either at home or at school or college, were entered as "Learning". Those who were not under instruction, but able both to read and write, were recorded as "Literate," and the remainder of the population as "Illiterate." It was found, however, that the return of the "Learning," was vitiated by the omission of children who had not long been at school, as they were entered as "Illiterate," and also of more advanced students, who were classed as "Literate". There were thus great discrepancies between the census return of the number of "Learning," and the corresponding statistics of the Education Department. It was therefore decided in 1901 to confine the entry in the enumeration schedules to the two main categories of "Literate" and "Illiterate", the former being those who were able both to read and write, and the latter those who did not satisfy this standard. No other criterion, however, was laid down, and the standard adopted, in deciding whether a person could read or write, was left indeterminate. At this census a further condition was imposed, viz., that a person was to be recorded as literate only if he could write a letter to a friend and read the answer to it. The standard was therefore higher than that hitherto prescribed, and if strictly applied, should have led to the exclusion of a number of persons who have previously been entered as literate, such as boys at school who can read and write a little, but are unable to write a letter, and also that large body of persons who can read, but have not got further with their writing than signing their names or keeping accounts.

That it has had some such effect (though not so much as it should have had) is apparent from the fact that in Calcutta the increase of literates among those under 15 years of age is 28 per cent., whereas it is 38 per cent. among those aged 15 and over, and that though the general population of the latter age has increased by only 4 per cent, whereas those under 15 have increased by $6\frac{1}{2}$ per cent.

General distribution of literacy.

84. In Calcutta and the Suburbs as a whole 298 out of every 1,000 persons can read and write, but there is a great difference in both the actual and proportional figures for the two sexes. There is only one literate female to every five males; and more than a third of the males are literate, but only one-seventh of the females. The results for Calcutta are moreover, very different from those for the Suburbs. In the former nearly one-third, but in the latter under one-sixth of the inhabitants have the elementary knowledge implied by the census test. These figures are far higher than in any other area in Bengal, as is only natural considering the number of educated Europeans, Bengalis, Marwaris and others in professional, commercial and clerical employment. That the general average of literacy is not even higher is due to the large proportion of uneducated labourers who flock into the metropolis for employment in manufacturing or industrial concerns or find casual labour sufficiently remunerative.

Locality.	Number of literates.		
	Total.	Male.	Female.
Calcutta	287,867	240,432	47,435
Suburbs	23,098	20,213	2,885
Total ...	310,965	260,645	50,320

Variations since 1901.

85. Since 1901 the number of literates in Calcutta has risen by 77,425, or 36 per cent., a remarkably rapid rate of growth when it is remembered that the population has had an addition of only 5·7 per cent. In the Suburbs, where the population has

grown by 45 per cent., there are now 9,370, or 68 per cent., more literates than there were 10 years ago. In the face of such figures as these, it cannot be said that the diffusion of education is failing to keep pace with the growth of the people. As in other parts of Bengal, the advance of education among females has been relatively greater than among males. The actual increase of female literates (15,957) in Calcutta and the Suburbs taken together is, it is true, only about one-fourth of that recorded for males (70,838), but proportionately it is greater, representing 46 per cent., compared with 37 per cent. for male literates.

LITERACY IN ENGLISH.

86 The last decade has witnessed a further dissemination of the knowledge of English, the number acquainted with that language rising by 43,549 or 48 per cent. It now aggregates 134,193, of whom all but 6,959 are resident in Calcutta itself.

Locality.	Literate in English.		
	Total.	Male.	Female.
Calcutta	127,234	111,131	16,103
Suburbs	6,959	6,517	442
Total ...	134,193	117,648	16,545

Here the number of males who have sufficient knowledge of English to be classed as literate amounts to 111,131 or about 37,000 more than in 1901, while the gentler sex can boast of 16,103 persons with the same proficiency, the actual increase in their case being nearly 3,600. Altogether, one in every six of the male, and one in every 18 of the female, inhabitants of the city are literate in English; and nearly half of the males and one-third of the females who can read and write have learnt to do so in that language. The denizens of the Suburbs are far less advanced, for there only one out of every 13 males and one out of every 129 females comes within the category of literate in English.

It must be remembered that these figures include Europeans and allied races, such as Australians, Canadians and Americans, besides Anglo-Indians and Armenians. If these be excluded, the number of males in Calcutta who are literate in English is reduced to 96,595, and of females to 5,707, while the Suburbs can claim only 6,185 Indian males and 257 Indian females with a similar knowledge.

LITERACY BY AGE.

87. The statistics of literacy by age present one curious feature. There is a steady rise in the proportional strength of male literates until the age of 20 is reached, but then the proportion, instead of rising as it would in a normally consitituted population, falls, viz., from 470 to 419 per mille in Calcutta, and from 283 to 25[illegible] per mille in the Suburbs. This curious phenomenon is the result of the influx of illiterate immigrants. A large number of those under 20 years of age are boys at school and students at college, whereas the majority of those above that age are foreign born labourers earning their daily bread. In the case of females the proportion of literates rises till the age of 15, but then declines slightly till the age of 20 is reached, after which there is a sharp drop, viz., from 6[illegible] to 166 per mille in Calcutta and from 95 to 49 in the Suburbs. The immigration of ignorant cooly women is only in a minor degree responsible for this. The chief cause is that the education of women being a development of comparatively recent times, the number of those who have received instruction is naturally greater among the younger generation. A secondary cause is that the education of a girl is rarely continued after she has left her home for her husband's house and undertaken the duties of married life.

LITERACY BY RELIGION.

88. Though the Christians represent only 4 per cent. of the population of Calcutta and the Suburbs, they contribute one-tenth of the literates. The magnitude of their share is, of course, due to the European element, for over three-fourths of the total number of literate Christians (32,424) are Europeans, Anglo-Indians, and Armenians. The share of the Hindus (73 per cent.) slightly exceeds their representation in the population (67 per cent.), whereas that of the Musalmans (14 per cent.) is far less than their proportional strength (29 per cent.)

The Brahmos are the most literate religious community, but are closely followed by the Parsis from Bombay, whose males are even more generally educated than those who have given their adherence to the Brahmo Samaj. Though the Christians occupy the third place, they have a higher proportion of female literates than any other religious body except the Brahmos; the general average among them is lowered by the Indian Christians, of whom 575 per mille are literate in Calcutta and 637 in the Suburbs. The Jews come fourth on the list; one-third of them are under 15 years of age, and the average among those aged 15 and over is no less than 790 per mille. The Jain males have a high place, but being mostly Marwari traders, brokers and agents, they do not consider it necessary that their females should be educated to the same extent; the ratio in the case of their women is as low as that of Hindu women. There is a similar disproportion in the case of the Sikhs, who are also immigrants. The average for the Hindus is lowered by the fact that they include so many immigrants drawn from the lower classes. Next to the Animists, who do not possess a single literate person, the Musalmans are by far the most ignorant, for among the males only one in five, and among the females only one in 31 has learnt to read and write.

RELIGION.	Total.	NUMBER OF LITERATES PER MILLE.	
		Male.	Female.
Brahmo	838	862	813
Parsi	823	871	743
Christian...	800	821	773
Jew	693	744	645
Jain	608	762	138
Buddhist	509	564	249
Sikh	501	588	88
Confucian	358	395	135
Hindu	327	422	138
Musalman	153	207	32
Animist	...	...	...

89. The statistics for race and caste, as distinct from religion, show that, excluding Europeans, the knowledge of reading and writing is most widely diffused among the Armenians, of whom nine-tenths are literate, while nearly as many are literate in English. The Anglo-Indians come next with a proportion of 84 per cent.; their males are slightly inferior to, but their females are more generally educated than, the Armenians. Both the Armenians and Anglo-Indians have improved their position since 1901, the proportion of literates among the former rising from 85 to 89 per cent., and among the latter from 76 to 84 per cent. Female education, in particular, has made great strides during the last decade among the Anglo-Indians and has raised the percentage of females who can read and write from 69 to 84. The Baidyas stand at the top of the Indian castes with 69 per cent. of literates; the second place is held by the Kayasths (60 per cent.), with the Brahmans (57 per cent.) in close proximity. These three castes also easily surpass all others in knowledge of English, over a fifth of their members being able to read and write that language. Both the foreign and indigenous trading castes have a fair average of literacy, viz., Agarwalas (41), Gandhabaniks (45), Oswals ($54\frac{1}{2}$) and Subarnabaniks (45). The figures for the Agarwalas and Oswals are remarkably high considering that education is almost confined to the males. It is obviously not thought worth while to educate girls who will not take an active part in business, and less than 4 per cent. of their females have received any education. The Bengali mercantile castes, *i.e*, the Gandhabaniks and Subarnabaniks, are more liberal, and the proportion of literate females among them is four times as great as among the foreign-born traders, though far lower than among the three castes first mentioned, viz., Baidya (49 per cent.), Kayasth (33 per cent.), and Brahman (27 per cent.). The Saiyads are the most advanced of the Musalman groups, but the standard they have reached is far below that attained by the Hindu castes already referred to. Of other castes the most literary are the Tambulis, Khatris, Sunris and Sadgops. The most ignorant are those which are rank low in the Hindu social scale, viz., Bagdi, Chamar, Dhoba, Dom, Dosadh, Kaora and Muchi. In none of them does the percentage of literates reach 10 per cent., while in the case of the Chamars, Doms, Kaoras and Muchis it falls below 5 per cent.

LITERACY BY RACE AND CASTE.

SUBSIDIARY TABLE I.—EDUCATION BY AGE, SEX AND RELIGION.

RELIGION.	Number per mille who are literate. All ages. Total.	All ages. Male.	All ages. Female.	0—10. Male.	0—10. Female.	10—15. Male.	10—15. Female.	15—20. Male.	15—20. Female.	20 and over. Male.	20 and over. Female.	Number per mille who are illiterate. Total.	Male.	Female.	Number per mille who are literate in English. Total.	Male.	Female.
CALCUTTA.																	
All Religions	***321***	***396***	***164***	***153***	***78***	***444***	***273***	***470***	***260***	***419***	***166***	***679***	***604***	***836***	***142***	***183***	***56***
Hindus	345	442	150	172	76	522	272	543	256	464	144	655	558	850	142	205	14
Muhammadans	170	222	37	46	14	191	59	248	64	246	38	830	778	963	40	54	3
Christians	801	822	774	405	373	873	906	852	894	909	866	199	178	226	729	755	696
Indian Christians ...	*575*	*592*	*558*	...	...	...	...	...	...	...	...	*425*	*408*	*447*	*354*	*389*	*308*
European and other Christians.	*889*	*910*	*869*	...	...	...	...	...	...	...	...	*111*	*90*	*138*	*876*	*895*	*849*
Brahmos	842	867	816	364	403	965	974	1,000	991	980	898	158	133	184	714	815	609
Buddhists	492	545	296	120	86	575	353	554	632	574	317	508	455	704	105	116	63
Animists	...	...	...	...	...	...	..	...	...	...	...	1,000	1,000	1,000	...	...	...
SUBURBS.																	
All Religions	***157***	***224***	***51***	***55***	***23***	***245***	***89***	***283***	***95***	***252***	***49***	***843***	***776***	***919***	***47***	***72***	***8***
Hindus	198	275	65	82	33	328	119	341	128	296	61	802	725	935	64	98	6
Muhammadans	82	127	17	24	5	132	32	164	36	154	18	918	873	983	11	19	1
Christians	763	774	748	200	328	636	964	778	732	946	922	237	226	252	630	725	518
Indian Christians ...	*637*	*513*	*746*	...	...	...	...	..	...	...	...	*363*	*487*	*254*	*265*	*349*	*191*
European and other Christians.	*827*	*879*	*780*	...		...	...	...	...	...	...	*173*	*121*	*250*	*817*	*876*	*780*
Brahmos	645	625	667	...	353	1,000	1,000	1,000	1,000	1,000	750	355	375	333	484	563	400
Buddhists	856	867	600	...	...	1,000		864	750	864	750	144	133	400	17	9	200
Animists	...	...	...	...	...	...	...	...	...	...	...	1,000	1,000	...	...	...	...

SUBSIDIARY TABLE II.—EDUCATION BY AGE, SEX AND LOCALITY.

	Number per mille who are literate. All ages. Total.	All ages. Male.	All ages. Female.	0—10. Male.	0—10. Female.	10—15. Male.	10—15. Female.	15—20. Male.	15—20. Female.	20 and over. Male.	20 and over. Female.
Calcutta 1911 ...	321	396	164	153	78	444	273	470	260	419	166
Calcutta 1901 ...	248	316	115	129	62	390	189	425	204	323	108
Suburbs 1911 ...	157	224	51	55	23	245	89	283	95	252	49
Suburbs 1901 ...	135	195	41	53	15	208	58	353	78	205	42

SUBSIDIARY TABLE III.—EDUCATION BY RELIGION, SEX AND LOCALITY.

	Number per mille who are literate. Hindu. Male.	Hindu. Female.	Musalman. Male.	Musalman. Female.	Christian. Male.	Christian. Female.	Buddhist. Male.	Buddhist. Female.	Brahmo. Male.	Brahmo. Female.
CALCUTTA AND SUBURBS.	***429***	***138***	***207***	***32***	***821***	***773***	***564***	***299***	***869***	***813***
Calcutta	442	150	222	37	822	774	545	296	867	816
Suburbs	275	65	127	17	774	748	867	600	625	667
Cossipur-Chitpur	279	68	108	10	781	773	875	1,000	750	714
Manicktollah ...	333	85	118	25	605	711	......	......	......	......
Garden Reach ...	187	25	147	14	915	638	905	500	250	......

SUBSIDIARY TABLE IV.—ENGLISH EDUCATION BY AGE, SEX AND LOCALITY.

	Literate in English per 10,000. 1911. 0—10. Male.	1911. 0—10. Female.	1911. 10—15. Male.	1911. 10—15. Female.	1911. 15—20. Male.	1911. 15—20. Female.	1911. 20 and over. Male.	1911. 20 and over. Female.	1911. All ages. Male.	1911. All ages. Female.	1901. All ages. Male.	1901. All ages. Female
CALCUTTA AND SUBURBS	***484***	***189***	***2,190***	***739***	***2,391***	***670***	***1,750***	***518***	***1,086***	***479***	***1,247***	***407***
Calcutta	564	222	2,414	853	2,475	776	1,883	604	1,829	558	1,322	455
Suburbs	86	26	818	126	1,107	130	802	83	723	78	564	58
Cossipur-Chitpur	70	37	740	236	1,104	210	850	122	754	120	532	91
Manicktollah	149	40	1,332	129	1,723	161	1,026	89	968	88	742	32
Garden Reach	29	...	320	27	433	29	504	35	406	25	336	46

SUBSIDIARY TABLE V.—Progress of Education.

	Number per mille who are literate.											
	All ages.				15—20.				20 and over.			
	Male.		Female.		Male.		Female.		Male.		Female.	
	1911.	1901.	1911.	1901.	1911.	1901.	1911.	1901.	1911.	1901.	1911.	1901.
CALCUTTA AND SUBURBS.	*373*	*304*	*146*	*106*	*449*	*417*	*233*	*189*	*398*	*312*	*146*	*100*
Calcutta	396	316	164	115	470	425	280	204	419	323	166	108
Suburbs	224	195	51	41	283	333	95	78	252	205	49	42
Cossipur-Chitpur ...	238	186	66	52	300	364	118	99	267	187	66	55
Manicktollah	254	223	62	40	358	405	130	87	277	228	56	36
Garden Reach ...	174	175	21	28	184	220	36	45	206	208	23	31

SUBSIDIARY TABLE VI—Education by Caste.

Calcutta and Suburbs.

Caste.	Number per 1,000 who are literate.						Number per 10,000 literate in English.					
	1911.			1901.			1911.			1901.		
	Total.	Male.	Female.	Total.	Male.	Female.	Total.	Male.	Female.	Total.	Male.	Female.
Hindu.												
Agarwala	415	627	39	401	557	42	439	672	25	180	259	...
Bagdi	75	148	8	41	89	9	148	302	1	101	195	2
Baidya	690	821	487	513	685	276	4,224	6,476	739	2,761	4,575	258
Baishnab	169	322	55	138	252	42	389	863	35	319	676	16
Brahman	572	713	266	464	598	187	2,706	3,831	271	2,077	3,015	140
Chamar	44	57	3	58	76	7	21	28	...	31	41	4
Chasi Kaibartta	226	341	45	188	268	5	632	1,011	35	483	737	21
Dhoba	79	110	2	62	89	14	220	347	8	84	129	5
Dom	32	54	2	49	80	5	12	21	...	9	15	...
Doaadh	61	79	15	86	121	10	74	108	7	68	98	4
Gandhabanik	449	653	147	319	507	62	1,484	2,401	139	1,047	1,783	38
Goala	172	208	58	161	208	39	349	441	60	274	373	18
Hujjam	144	166	...	Not available.			237	273	...	Not available.		
Jaliya Kaibartta	137	223	36		...	..	216	369	34	...	...	...
Kahar	115	142	12	114	141	23	105	130	6	51	65	6
Kamar	312	456	103	254	384	58	545	1,386	56	618	1,011	26
Kansari	355	615	78	218	383	49	1,432	2,721	64	421	805	31
Kaora	43	77	8	30	41	19	35	69	...	16	33	
Kayasth	596	755	328	479	610	252	3,218	4,906	361	2,397	3,663	218
Khatri	408	498	181	277	374	74	994	1,288	104	475	694	27
Mali	283	373	90	Not available.			839	1,161	147	Not available.		
Mayra	314	403	110	239	324	54	790	1,066	114	486	688	47
Muchi	43	57	5	27	35	3	91	124	8	7	8	4
Napit	224	308	72	203	284	46	578	863	28	543	822	4
Oswal	545	714	27	493	649	61	605	802	...	112	150	...
Rajput	369	425	89	307	368	45	655	772	75	205	250	11
Sadgop	304	606	120	355	565	103	1,647	2,863	76	1,196	2,158	51
Sonar	182	248	36	210	301	28	324	467	...	131	188	13
Subarnabanik	450	680	164	311	509	77	2,171	3,837	103	1,464	2,639	70
Sunri	431	598	90	347	490	45	1,523	2,228	94	1,081	1,578	37
Sutradhar	272	391	111	179	259	55	1,031	1,757	37	606	973	41
Swarnakar	276	419	9	204	295	47	696	1,104	97	592	925	18
Tambuli	463	712	90	216	299	41	1,618	2,362	96	642	933	29
Tanti	296	460	111	205	322	66	1,317	2,418	81	858	1,544	42
Teli	293	394	80	230	332	61	880	1,231	92	565	896	13
Musalman.												
Pathan	216	265	50	165	199	49	517	664	33	267	337	33
Saiyad	310	384	117	233	295	79	1,086	1,475	85	569	794	14
Sheikh	125	172	24	111	150	26	263	376	17	169	239	10
Christian.												
Anglo-Indian	841	845	837	764	840	691	8,267	8,361	8,177	7,640	8,398	6,908
Armenian	891	939	820	851	931	724	8,818	9,189	7,788	8,510	9,312	7,181
Brahmo.												
Brahmo	838	862	813	613	664	531	7,090	8,101	6,052	4,669	4,281	3 781
Jew.												
Jew	693	744	645	554	667	448	6,005	6,542	5,497	4,367	4,875	3,889

CHAPTER IX.

INFIRMITIES.

Introductory.

90. As at previous censuses, four infirmities have been recorded, viz., insanity, deaf-mutism from birth, total blindness and leprosy. The instructions to the enumerators regarding the record of infirmities were that only persons who are blind of both eyes, or insane, or suffering from corrosive leprosy, or deaf and dumb from birth were to be entered in the schedules, and that those who were blind of one eye, or suffering from white leprosy only, or who had become deaf and dumb after birth were to be excluded.

General distribution.

91. Altogether 1,783 persons were returned as suffering from one or more of these infirmities, of whom 14 unfortunate beings were doubly afflicted, *i.e.*, suffered both from insanity or leprosy, or from insanity and deaf-mutism, or were both blind and lepers, or were blind and deaf-mutes, or were deaf-mutes and lepers. The number of the afflicted returned at this and the last census, and their distribution between Calcutta and the Suburbs, are shown in the marginal statement, from which it will be seen that, in spite of the increase of population, there is a decrease in every case except leprosy.

Infirmity.	Calcutta.	Suburbs.	Total	
			1911.	1901.
Insane ...	328	85	413	501
Deaf-mutes ...	275	50	325	376
Blind ...	650	116	766	779
Lepers ...	271	22	293	260

Insanity.

92. The number of insane persons enumerated is inflated by the concentration of lunatics in the Bhawanipore Lunatic Asylum: excluding those inmates who have come from outside Calcutta, the proportion of insane persons per 100,000 of the total population of Calcutta is only 36 for males and 29 for females, which is far below the proportion for Bengal, viz., 50 for males and 36 for females. One-seventh of the persons returned as insane are Europeans and Anglo-Indians, but the high proportion in their case is due mainly to the fact that the Bhawanipore Lunatic Asylum is intended for persons belonging to either of those communities, and that Europeans and Anglo-Indians who have lost their reason are sent there from all over Bengal, Bihar and Orissa. Of Indian castes, the Brahmans, Kayasths and Sheikhs have the largest number of lunatics: proportionately, the Kayasths are the most afflicted of the three, 50 per 100,000 being insane, and then the Brahmans with a proportion of 35, and the Sheikhs with 30.

Deaf-mutism.

93. The incidence of deaf-mutism is far lower than in Bengal, and it is probable that the figures should be even lower than they are, for a certain number of elderly persons have been entered in the returns who were almost certainly suffering from senile deafness. Deaf-mutes are, as a rule, short-lived and these entries are in all probability due to the enumeraters having misunderstood the rules and entered persons who were only deaf.

Locality.	No. per 100,000	
	Male.	Female.
Calcutta ...	28	35
Suburbs ...	40	25
Bengal ...	81	58

Blindness.

94. The most noticeable features of the returns for blind persons are (1) that the incidence of blindness among males is lower, but among females is far higher, than in the province of which Calcutta is the capital, and (2) that loss of sight is less frequent among men than among women, whereas the reverse is the case in Bengal. The explanation of this phenomenon is twofold. In the first place males suffering from cataract have recourse to the surgeon more freely than women—an examination of the returns for 16,500 successful operations for cataract

Locality.	No. per 100,000	
	Male.	Female.
Calcutta ...	68	92
Suburbs ...	62	105
Bengal ...	78	6[illegible]

in Bengal, Bihar and Orissa during 1901-10 shows that 3 males are operated on to every 2 females. In the second place, the life which women have to lead renders them more liable to have their sight impaired. Their work lies mainly in the house, and a large proportion have to spend their days in small dark rooms filled with the acrid smoke of cowdung fires, at which they cook their food. The accumulative effect of life under such conditions is apparent from the returns of blindness by age, for two-thirds of the blind women are over 50 years of age. The village homesteads are far better ventilated, as the bamboo walls and roofs allow of a more thorough perflation of air; the Bengali woman in the village consequently suffers less than her sister in the metropolis. The *purdah* woman is particularly liable to suffer from the effects of confinement to the house, especially in congested areas. To quote from a report by Dr. H. M. Crake on the sanitary condition of the northern portion of Calcutta: "No survey of an Oriental city can possibly ignore the potent influence of the *purdah* system on its domestic architecture. Obviously, the house is directly inspired by the necessity of securing absolute privacy for the ladies of the household. To effectually seclude the inner apartments from the vulgar gaze, air and light are shut out and the rooms rendered unfit for human habitation. It is very common to find the whole of the lower storey of the zanana, even in large and valuable houses, given up to godowns and kitchens, the inmates frankly admitting that none of the rooms are fit to live in. I must confess I am astonished at the average kitchen. It is, in a large number of houses, a gloomy, stuffy den, full of acrid smoke, and yet the ladies of the house have to spend hours in these very unpleasant surroundings. The entire absence of chimneys results in an atmosphere which is almost unbearable when cooking is going on in a particularly ill-ventilated kitchen." No less than 232 persons, or one-third of the blind, are Musalman Sheikhs, which seems *primâ facie* a large proportion, but it must be remembered that they constitute over one-fourth of the total population and that many of them observe the *purdah* system.

95. Since 1901 there has been a small increase in the number of lepers, amounting to 33, viz., 19 males and 14 females. The increase is not of much account, for the population has grown, and there is always a natural tendency for these unfortunate beings to come into a large city in search of charity. In spite of the increase, the general incidence of leprosy is lower than in Bengal, except as regards females in Calcutta. There, however, the average is artificially raised by the presence of the leper asylum at Gobra: if the inmates who were born outside Calcutta are left out of account, the proportion per 100,000 females is only 20, which is very little above the mean ratio for Bengal, while the average for males is reduced to 18 per 100,000. No less than 73 lepers, or one quarter of the total number are Indian Christians, but, as explained in the last census report, conversion to Christianity on the appearance of symptoms of leprosy is not infrequent, the leper being assured of finding pity and protection in the Christian community. The Sheikhs count amongst them 62 lepers, or over one-fifth, but this is not incommensurate with their proportional representation in the population.

LEPROSY

Locality.	No. per 100,000	
	Male.	Female.
Calcutta ...	32	26
Suburbs ...	19	9
Bengal ...	56	19

SUBSIDIARY TABLE I.—Number afflicted per 100,000 of the population at each of the last three Censuses.

Calcutta and Suburbs.	Insane.						Deaf-mute.						Blind.						Lepers.					
	Male.			Female.			Male.			Female.			Male.			Female.			Male.			Female.		
	1911.	1901.	1891.	1911.	1901.	1891.	1911.	1901.	1891.	1911.	1901.	1891.	1911.	1901.	1891.	1911.	1901.	1891.	1911.	1901.	1891.	1911.	1901.	1891.
1	2	3	4	5	6	7	8	9	10	11	12	13	14	15	16	17	18	19	20	21	22	23	24	25
Calcutta	39	60	71	33	49	49	28	37	24	35	44	42	63	70	88	92	105	60	32	32	26	26	22	25
Suburbs	68	27	*	40	26	*	40	30	*	25	43	*	62	69	*	105	102	*	19	22	*	9	10	*

* Not available.

SUBSIDIARY TABLE II.—Number afflicted per 100,000 persons of each age-period and number of females afflicted per 1,000 males.

Age.	Number afflicted per 100,000.								Number of females afflicted per 1,000 males.			
	Insane.		Deaf-mute.		Blind.		Lepers.		Insane.	Deaf-mute.	Blind.	Lepers.
	Male.	Female.	Male.	Female.	Male.	Female.	Male.	Female.				
1	2	3	4	5	6	7	8	9	10	11	12	13
Calcutta.												
0—5	3	...	34	13	25	...	8	...	...	364	...	...
5—10	11	...	54	56	54	13	8	...	...	947	211	...
10—15	12	16	58	33	46	37	14	...	800	320	450	...
15—20	30	11	39	46	25	4	11	11	176	545	71	500
20—25	26	32	20	39	25	32	7	10	455	706	476	500
25—30	39	42	16	31	30	55	38	8	348	645	693	294
30—35	47	32	22	39	33	47	37	25	237	611	481	283
35—40	44	64	15	52	42	46	29	76	476	1,125	364	367
40—45	56	84	23	33	75	98	66	47	621	583	538	294
45—50	56	87	34	10	94	146	56	29	450	125	652	231
50—55	72	55	40	21	160	220	96	62	444	300	800	375
55—60	118	54	34	...	147	217	79	36	300	...	923	286
60 and over ...	53	37	27	43	500	662	84	80	583	1,333	1,097	789
All ages ..	*39*	*33*	*28*	*35*	*63*	*99*	*39*	*96*	*409*	*590*	*688*	*383*
Suburbs.												
0—5	...	31	45	...	60	63	...	...	...	...	1,000	...
5—10	...	...	141	92	56	31	...	...	...	600	500	...
10—15	42	...	84	44	56	22	14	...	...	333	250	...
15—20	28	39	42	39	84	19	...	...	1,000	667	167	...
20—25	96	15	9	...	17	30	...	...	91	...	1,000	...
25—30	118	71	17	...	17	36	5	...	286	...	1,000	...
30—35	88	104	44	52	18	86	26	...	600	600	2,500	...
35—40	44	65	29	...	44	65	44	33	667	...	667	333
40—45	50	99	...	25	25	74	38	...	1,000	...	1,500	...
45—50	288	52	...	...	89	155	30	...	125	...	1,000	...
50—55	26	37	103	...	26	220	26	78	1,000	...	6,000	2,000
55—60	...	...	...	...	154	190	77	...	...	...	1,000	...
60 and over ...	25	140	...	...	518	759	74	56	5,000	..	1,286	667
All ages ...	*63*	*49*	*40*	*95*	*62*	*105*	*19*	*9*	*491*	*389*	*1,071*	*994*

SUBSIDIARY TABLE III.—Distribution of the infirm by age per 10,000 of each sex.

Age.	Insane. Male. 1911.	Insane. Male. 1901.	Insane. Male. 1891.	Insane. Female. 1911.	Insane. Female. 1901.	Insane. Female. 1891.	Deaf-mute. Male. 1911.	Deaf-mute. Male. 1901.	Deaf-mute. Male. 1891.	Deaf-mute. Female. 1911.	Deaf-mute. Female. 1901.	Deaf-mute. Female. 1891.	Blind. Male. 1911.	Blind. Male. 1901.	Blind. Male. 1891.	Blind. Female. 1911.	Blind. Female. 1901.	Blind. Female. 1891.	Lepers. Male. 1911.	Lepers. Male. 1901.	Lepers. Male. 1891.	Lepers. Female. 1911.	Lepers. Female. 1901.	Lepers. Female. 1891.
1	2	3	4	5	6	7	8	9	10	11	12	13	14	15	16	17	18	19	20	21	22	23	24	25
Calcutta																								
0—5	43	30	126	...	144	261	636	333	561	393	80	506	208	202	351	...	167	213	51	...	174	...	...	345
5—10	171	60	126	...	216	74	1,098	905	841	1,765	1,040	707	494	177	234	161	67	213	51	56	174	...	161	345
10—15	214	239	126	426	492	435	1,445	1,048	561	784	1,040	909	520	328	585	340	166	355	306	111	348	...	161	862
15—20	726	269	377	319	791	522	1,272	952	936	1,177	1,280	202	364	556	585	38	367	71	306	667	435	400	323	517
20—25	940	1,493	1,038	1,064	1,223	34	983	1,143	935	1,177	800	404	545	404	468	377	333	284	306	1,000	783	400	968	862
25—30	1,496	1,791	1,509	1,277	935	78	809	905	841	882	640	404	701	758	351	604	333	149	1,735	1,333	869	1,333	645	...
30—35	1,684	1,642	1,447	957	1,367	522	1,041	763	1,215	1,079	400	1,010	701	1,439	468	491	467	567	1,531	1,222	1,130	934	1,290	862
35—40	983	1,731	1,635	1,170	1,079	2,522	462	619	934	888	480	505	571	328	585	302	400	142	765	1,111	1,826	1,733	1,613	517
40—45	1,289	895	1,164	1,915	1,367	1,217	694	857	654	686	720	1,111	1,013	1,111	818	794	833	993	1,735	1,333	1,478	1,333	1,129	862
45—50	855	478	1,006	957	1,007	1,217	462	571	654	93	320	606	571	631	702	566	433	851	663	667	528	400	323	1,035
50—55	769	537	503	881	504	956	578	667	654	294	720	808	1,039	783	1,286	1,207	967	1,489	1,225	1,167	696	1,200	968	690
55—60	487	328	566	319	288	608	173	286	467	..	320	1,414	338	379	2,748	453	667	2,269	357	333	435	267	1,935	1,724
60 and over	513	507	377	745	647	435	347	952	748	784	2,160	1,415	2,835	2,904	819	4,679	4,800	2,411	969	1,000	1,130	2,000	484	1,379
Total ...	10,000	10,000	10,000	10,000	10,000	10,000	10,000	10,000	10,000	10,000	10,000	10,000	10,000	10,000	10,000	10,000	10,000	10,000	10,000	10,000	10,000	10,000	10,000	10,000
Suburbs.			Not available.			Not available.			Not available.			Not available.			Not available.			Not available.			Not available.			Not available.
0—5	...	...		714	...		833	833		...	1,177		714	232		667	500		...	...		...	...	
5—10	...	...		...	...		3,778	...		4,286	1,176		714	465		334	...		...	...		...	...	
10—15	526	...		...	1,000		1,667	2,500		1,429	1,177		714	465		167	..		588	714		...	...	
15—20	351	1,177		714	...		833	...		1,428	...		1,072	830		167	...		...	...		...	...	
20—25	1,930	2,383		357	1,000		278	833		...	588		357	233		333	250		...	714		...	...	
25—30	2,456	2,941		1,429	2,000		556	417		...	1,765		357	232		333	250		588	715		...	...	
30—35	1,754	1,176		2,143	2,000		1,389	833		2,143	588		357	698		833	750		1,765	714		...	...	
35—40	526	1,177		714	1,000		556	834		...	...		536	698		333	1,000		1,765	714		2,000	2,500	
40—45	709	...		1,429	1,000		...	833		714	588		357	930		500	500		1,765	1,429		...	2,500	
45—50	1,404	588		357	...		...	417		...	...		536	465		500	500		588	...		...	...	
50—55	176	...		357	2,000		1,111	1,250		...	1,177		179	233		1,000	1,750		588	1,429		4,000	2,500	
55—60	...	588		...	...		...	417		...	588		357	...		333	750		588	...		...	2,500	
60 and over	175	...		1,786	...		...	833		...	1,176		3,750	4,419		4,500	3,750		1,765	3,571		4,000	...	
Total ...	10,000	10,000		10,000	10,000		10,000	10,000		10,000	10,000		10,000	10,000		10,000	10,000		10,000	10,000		10,000	10,000	

CHAPTER X.

OCCUPATIONS.

INTRODUCTORY.

96. THE statistics on which the discussion in this chapter is based will be found in Tables XV and XVI. Table XV is divided into the following five parts. Part A is a general summary, showing the number of persons following the different occupations entered in the prescribed scheme of classification. Part B shows the subsidiary occupations followed by persons whose main occupation is agriculture. Part C is an optional table, giving statistics of combined occupations, which has not been compiled. Part D shows the distribution of occupations by religion. Part E embodies the results of the industrial census, *i.e.*, a census of industrial concerns employing 20 persons or more, which was held concurrently with the general census. The first section shows the number of persons employed in each kind of industry, distinguishing between industrial concerns in which mechanical power is used and those in which it is not, and classifying them according to the number employed. The other two sections show the castes and races of the owners and managers. In Table XVI statistics are given of the occupations of selected castes and races. The occupations are arranged under 13 main heads corresponding to the sub-classes of the scheme of classification; these heads have been subdivided, where necessary, in order to distinguish between different occupations. As usual, the tables are supplemented by subsidiary tables, dealing with the more salient features of the returns, which are given at the end of the chapter.

INDUSTRIAL CENSUS.

THE SCOPE OF THE INDUSTRIAL CENSUS.

97. The general tables of occupations, while they indicate the main functional distribution of the people, furnish meagre information regarding individual manufactures and industries, and throw little light on recent industrial developments. An attempt, it is true, was made in 1901 to distinguish between workers in factories and those engaged in home industries, and also to distinguish, in the case of factories, between "Owners, managers and superior staff" and "Operatives," but the entries in the schedules were far too vague to permit of accurate information on these points being obtained. In order to remedy this defect, the Census Commissioner recommended that, in addition to the general and household schedules, a special schedule should be prescribed for persons working in mills, factories, etc., and this proposal was accepted by the Government of India. It was decided that the schedules, or, as they should more properly be called, the returns, should be filled in for all industrial or manufacturing works in which at least 20 persons were employed at the time of the census.

98. The returns, which were filled in by the owners, agents or managers, and not by the census staff, specified the character of the mill, factory, etc., *e.g.*, whether it was a jute mill, or jute press, or cotton mill, the nature of the mechanical power employed, and the state of the trade or industry when the census was taken. They further stated the castes or nationalities of owners and managers, and recorded the number of persons in superior employ, of skilled workmen and unskilled workmen, those last mentioned being divided into two classes, viz., persons over and under 14 years of age. The statistics compiled from these returns therefore furnish information not only regarding the number of persons employed in different manufactures and industries, but also regarding the extent to which indigenous enterprise takes its share in various industrial undertakings, and the sections of the community to which the owners and managers belong in each class of industry. Briefly, they throw light on the industrial development of the city, and,

in spite of the scientific classification of occupations returned at the general census, are of greater value than the statistics entered in the general table of occupations, so far as industries and manufactures are concerned.

99. At the same time, it must be remembered that the returns refer to the state of affairs on a particular day of the year when some concerns were closed, others were not in full work, and others again had a larger number of operatives than usual. Some concerns work only for a period of the year; if they were not at work on the date of the census, they were necessarily excluded from the returns. In other cases the busy manufacturing season comes after or before the census date, so that the number of employés returned does not represent the full labour force. Conversely, of course, the busy season may be synchronous with the date of the census, in which case the number of persons employed is greater than at other times of the year. Apart moreover from the question of manufacturing seasons, the strength of the labour force depends on the state of trade and the demand for manufactured goods in particular industries, which may be normal, or brisk, or dull in varying degrees.

100. Calcutta and the Suburbs contain 572 industrial and manufacturing concerns employing 20 hands or more, or two-fifths of the aggregate for the whole Province. The number of employés is 78,890, which represents 8 per cent. of the population and 13 per cent. of the total returned for Bengal. More than half of these (40,225) are skilled workmen, of whom all but 442 are Indians. Those engaged in direction, supervision and clerical work number 5,531; altogether 1,106, or one-fifth, are Europeans and Anglo-Indians. The unskilled labourers, of whom there are 33,134, include 3,797 females and 2,638 children under 14 years of age.

LOCALITY.	Number of concerns.	Employés.
Calcutta	495	63,471
Cossipur-Chitpur ...	48	10,092
Manicktollah	18	3,019
Garden Reach	11	2,308
Total ...	572	78,890

101. The marginal statement of the principal concerns shows how largely the jute industry predominates, jute mills and presses furnishing employment to over 20,000 persons. Next in importance come printing presses, which are more numerous than any other kind of concern: the number of hands shown as employed in printing presses is swollen by the inclusion of those belonging to the Government of India Press, which was located in Calcutta at the time of the census. Other large concerns owned by Government are the Telegraph Workshops with 847 workers and the Mint with 922. One new industry of growing importance is the repair of motor-cars. Though motor-cars have only recently been introduced, there were nearly 1,000 men employed in motor-car works at the time of the census. It is interesting also to note that the Indians are no longer content to allow foreign countries to supply them with umbrellas and have started 14 works for their manufacture, in which 656 persons are employed.

WORKS.	Number.	Employés.
Jute mills	6	15,111
Printing presses ...	99	11,880
Jute presses	24	5,972
Dockyards and Port Commissioners' workshops.	3	5,130
Machinery and engineering works.	20	3,692
Gas and electric light works	5	3,298
Oil mills	90	3,032
Cotton mills	4	3,114

OWNERS.

102. Excluding the municipal concerns and works belonging to Government, and including both private and company-owned concerns, there are 367 owned by Indians, 179 by Europeans and Anglo-Indians, 4 by members of both communities, and 7 by Chinese. Some branches of industry and manufacture are entirely or almost entirely monopolized by the Indian community, *e.g*, they own all or nearly all the rope works, timber yards, type foundries, brass foundries, oil mills, soap factories, chemical works, flour mills, rice mills, sugar factories, umbrella manufactories, *surki* factories, etc. They also own the greater number

of the iron foundries and iron and steel works, jute presses and printing presses, and have a considerable interest in chemical works, but theyhave no share in such important concerns as jute mills and very little in machinery and engineering works. The works belonging to the Chinese are all concerned either with carpentry and woodwork, or with the boot and shoe trade. Altogether 105, or over a sixth of the various undertakings, are controlled by companies, of which only seven have Indians as directors; four more have boards of which the directors are partly of Indian and partly of European or Anglo-Indian origin. The seven companies, of which the directors are entirely Indian, own 2 chemical works, 1 pencil factory, 1 cigarette factory, 1 bicycle factory and 2 printing presses. The European companies own all the jute mills, all but one of the cotton mills, 10 jute presses, 11 printing preses and 12 machinery and engineering works.

Among private owners there are 380 Indians to 85 Europeans and Anglo-Indians. In other words, there are about four Indians to every one European or Anglo-Indian. The castes from which these private owners are mainly drawn are the Kayasths (65), and Brahmans (61), each of them accounting for about one-sixth of the total number, and then *longo inte vallo* the Telis and Tilis (28) and Sadgops (26). The Kalus come next on the list, having 20 oil presses, but no other works in their possession. Though the Sheikhs number over a quarter of a million, only 18 of them are found in the list of owners, or less than those shrewd and enterprising foreign merchants, the Marwaris (19). Of indigenous Bengali castes, the Baidyas claim 16 and the Chasi Kaibarttas 12, but the Subarnabaniks only 10 private owners : none of them is in this respect on the same level as the Sadgop.

MANAGERS.

103. The races and castes of managers are naturally very much the same as those of the owners. Of the 572 works that came within the purview of the industrial census, 202 are managed by Europeans and Anglo-Indians, 364 by Indians and 7 by Chinese. Indians manage all or nearly all the rope works, brass foundries, oil mills, timber yards, soap factories, chemical works, flour mills, sugar factories, cigarette factories, umbrella factories, *surki* factories, and book-binding workshops. They further manage the greater number of the iron foundries and iron and steel works, two-thirds of the printing presses, and one-third of the jute presses. On the other hand, they furnish few or none of the managers of the jute mills, machinery and engineering works, tailoring workshops, confectionery works, coach building works, motor-car works, scientific, optical and musical intrument workshops, ice factories, gas and electric light works, etc., the staff of which is entirely or mainly manned by Europeans and Anglo-Indians. The Kayasths and Brahmans head the list of Indian managers just as they do that of the Indian owners, and then in order come the Sadgops, Sheikhs, and Telis and Tilis. The Marwaris evidently prefer or have to employ strangers as managers, for though there are 19 Marwari owners, only eight Marwaris are retained in the post of manager.

GENERAL CENSUS.

GENERAL DISTRIBUTION OF OCCUPATIONS.

104. In Calcutta and the Suburbs 253,320 persons, or one-fourth of the population, are supported by industrial occupations, and 190,836, or nearly one-fifth, by trade. Transport furnishes a means of livelihood to 126,330 or 12 per cent., while those who are maintained by the public administration and the liberal arts number only 3,000 less. Of those entered under the latter head 10,798 belong to the army and the police, or are dependent on soldiers and policemen, and 34,680 subsist by employment in the public administration; the remainder, who aggregate 56,075, have occupations connected with religion, the professions (such as law, medicine and education), letters, arts and sciences. Domestic service accounts for no less than 117,763, or 11 per cent. of the inhabitants, while 161,601 come under the head of "Insufficiently described occupations." Nearly half the latter are "Labourers and workmen otherwise unspecified," who correspond to general labourers.

There are 39,036 persons, or 4 per cent., who are dependent on pasture and agriculture, and 21,571 live on their income. The number of those who come under the category of unproductive occupations is 28,732, of whom 24,155 are beggars, vagrants and prostitutes.

105. The diagram given below exhibits in a graphic form the general distribution of occupations in Calcutta. The distribution is much the same in the Suburbs, except that the industrial population has relatively a larger, and the commercial population a smaller, representation, the proportions which they bear to the total population being 44 and 25½ per cent., respectively, whereas they are 21 and 31 per cent. in Calcutta. The detailed figures may now be briefly reviewed, the same order being followed as in the table of occupations:—

GENERAL DISTRIBUTION OF THE POPULATION BY OCCUPATION (SUB-CLASSES)

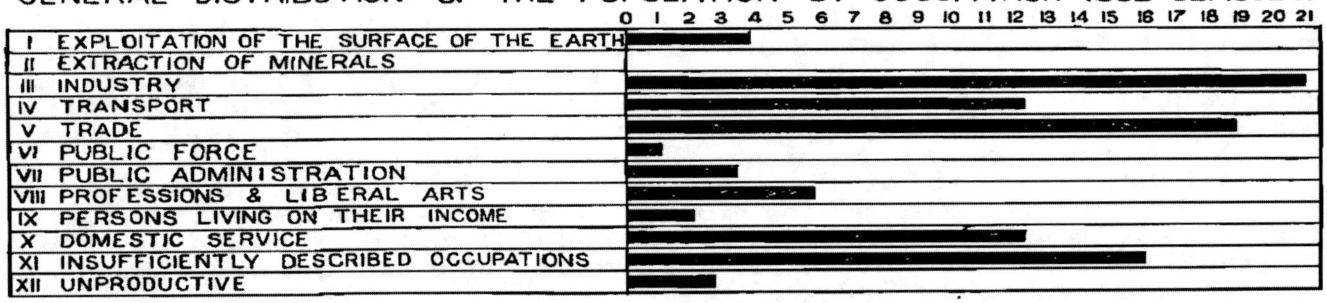

Pasture and agriculture.

106. It seems at first sight a little surprising that in a great commercial and industrial city as many as 39,036 persons should be dependent on pasture and agriculture for a means of livelihood. The explanation is partly that a number or those enumerated in Calcutta are temporary residents, who work there only for few a months and cultivate their fields during the remainder of the year. Their principal means of livelihood is therefore returned as cultivation, and not the occupation they may actually follow at the time of the census. Even the factory operative is generally a cultivator and only a periodic worker in the mills. As stated in the report of the Indian Factory Labour Commission of 1907-08:—"The habits of the Indian factory operative are determined by the fact that he is primarily an agriculturist, or a labourer on the land. In almost all cases his hereditary occupation is agriculture; his home is in the village from which he comes, not in the city in which he labours; his wife and family ordinarily continue to live in that village; he regularly remits a portion of his wages there; and he returns there periodically to look after his affairs. The Indian operative is, in general, independent of factory work, to the extent that he does not rely exclusively upon factory employment in order to obtain a livelihood." The greater number, however, of those who are shown as dependent on pasture and agriculture are maintained by the income received from the rent of agricultural land. Their actual number is 23,255, of whom 7,288 are returned as workers, *i.e.*, are actual landlords. The remainder consist of persons dependent on them, *i.e.*, their families or boys who have been sent to Calcutta to receive an education. The actual landlords represent about one-thirtieth of the landlords of Bengal, from which it may be inferred that there is ground for the complaints about absentee proprietors who prefer the amenities of Calcutta to life on their estates. This tendency is obviously growing, for the number of landlords enumerated in Calcutta and the suburbs is 1,645 more than in 1901.

Industry.

107. Nearly one-sixth of the industrial population consists of workers in textile industries and their families. The majority of those returned under this latter head are jute spinners and weavers, who aggregate 34,023, a greater number than is returned for any other single industrial occupation. Industries of the dress and toilet provide for even more than the textile industries, supplying 63,277 persons

with their daily bread ; of these 26,351 are tailors and dress-makers and their families, 18,144 are shoe and boot-makers, 9,691 are those useful members of society, the washermen, and 6,868 are barbers. The miscellaneous occupations classified as "Industries of luxury and those pertaining to literature and the arts and sciences" maintain 38,501 persons, nearly all of whom are printers and lithographers 1?,596) and jewellers, goldsmiths, silversmiths, etc., (15,501). Next in importance come building industries, which support 35,123 persons, or nearly one-seventh of the industrial population. Lastly, the humble but indispensable class of sweepers and scavengers numbers 15,381, or a little under one-third of all those enumerated in Bengal: nearly 9,000 of them are actual workers.

TRANSPORT.

108. Transport is an important means of livelihood, for it includes all those who subsist by work on the roads and railways as well as on the water. Transport by water, *i.e.*, work in the *Port* or on the *Canals*, accounts for no less than 52,559 persons, or 5 per cent. of the total population: four-fifths of this number are workers, *i.e.*, are actually engaged in work either in the dockyards, or on steamers, ships, country-boats, flats, barges, etc. The railways maintain 19,514 persons, or about one-third as many as the Port and Canals, while 42,645 persons subsist by work on the roads, *e.g.*, as cart and carriage owners, carters, coachmen, stable-boys, etc. (excluding private servants). It is curious to note that 1,000 persons still depend on that primitive means of conveyance, the *p ilki*, for their livelihood.

TRADE.

109. Of the commercial population, 72,018, or nearly two-fifths, are engaged in purveying food. The actual number is really greater, for 14,737 persons returned themselves simply as shopkeepers without specifying the articles which they sold, and a large proportion of these must have been vendors of food stuffs. Trade in textiles provides for 24,263 persons, while 7,935 sell clothing and toilet articles. Nearly 22,000 follow the higher branches of commerce, *i.e.*, work in banks, insurance companies and exchange agencies, or are brokers, commission agents, and warehouse owners, or their employés.

PUBLIC FORCE AND ADMINISTRATION.

110. The heading Public Force includes persons serving in the army, navy and police and those supported by them. At the time of the census there were 4,263 soldiers in Calcutta, and 5,850 returned service in the police as their principal means of livelihood: the number of the latter does not necessarily correspond to the actual number in the ranks of the police, for it includes 1,257 dependants, and a constable may get a larger income from landed property than from his wages, in which case he will come under the head of Agriculture. Calcutta being the head-quarters of the Government of Bengal, and also of the Government of India at the time of the census, the number returned as members of the public administration was naturally large. Altogether 9,334 were in State service, and nearly twice as many (17,305) were supported by them. The number of dependants is naturally swollen by the fact that many Government servants have their homes in Calcutta, and others send their children there to be educated. Municipal service under the Calcutta Corporation or under the Suburban Municipal Boards supports about 8,000 persons.

111. The marginal statement shows the number of those who obtain a livelihood from the professions and the liberal arts. It must not be imagined that they all occupy a high position in the professional, literary or scientific world. There is one clerk, petition-writer or tout to every two lawyers; a quarter of the medical profession are midwives, nurses, compounders, etc.; and of those who come under the head of "Letters, arts and sciences" over one-fourth are musicians, singers, actors and dancers, often of a low order. The

PROFESSIONS AND LIBERAL ARTS.

	Number supported.	Workers.
Religion	15,548	8,194
Law	10,800	3,016
edicine	11,800	4,233
Instruction	7,196	3,316
Letters, arts and sciences ...	9,932	4,491

legal profession has gained many fresh recruits during the last 10 years, and the number of those, who are able to make a living as lawyers and barristers, vakils and mukhtars has increased by 605, or 45 per cent., bringing up the total to 1,947. There are now 2,741 medical practitioners, including 83 women, and 1,713 architects, surveyors, engineers and their employés. The number of persons engaged in other literary and scientific pursuits, such as authors, artists, sculptors, astronomers, meteorologists, botanists and photographers, is small, aggregating only 797.

MISCELLANEOUS.

112. Among those actually employed in domestic service, whether as indoor or outdoor servants *e.g.*, as cooks, bearers, khitmatgars, coachmen, syces and maid servants), there are three males to every female. The aggregate of persons coming under the head "Insufficiently described occupations" is even greater than that of domestic service. This latter head includes all those who described themselves as manufacturers, business men, contractors, clerks, artisans, labourers, etc., without mentioning any particular branch of commerce and industry.

PROSTITUTES.

113. The number returned as beggars, vagrants and prostitutes is noticeably large, viz., 24,155, of whom 4,044 are dependants. In this category there are 5 females to every male. The disparity of the sexes is due to the very large number of prostitutes, which amounts to 14,271, viz., 12,848 in Calcutta and 1,423 in the Suburbs. Large as this number is, it is 4,049 less than was returned in 1901.

The prostitutes of Calcutta represent 4½ per cent. of the total female population, and 21 per cent. of the women who returned themselves as engaged in any occupation. The percentage calculated on the total female population, however, gives a misleading idea of the proportion of prostitutes, as it includes girls under 10 years of age, who are not old enough for a life of shame. Excluding them, we find that 6 per cent. of the females of Calcutta are professional prostitutes: the actual number is probably even greater, for it is not every prostitute who is hardened enough to proclaim herself such, and many describe themselves euphemistically as maid-servants The proportion is even higher among women aged 20 to 40, among whom one in every 12 is a woman of ill-fame. It may be added that no less than 1,096 girls under 10 years of age (997 in Calcutta and 99 in the Suburbs) were returned as dependants on prostitutes, and it may fairly be assumed that they are being brought up to the same profession.

Special statistics of the castes and nationalities of the 14,271 prostitutes in Calcutta and the Suburbs show that ninetenths are Hindus, and that 2,962, or over one-fifth, are Kaibarttas. The Baishnabs contribute 1,770, the Kayasths 1,408, the Sadgops 844, and the Musalman Sheikhs 803; one out of every 5 Baishnab females retured herself as a professional prostitute. Only 22 are Europeans or members of allied races, while 49 are Jewesses and 55 Japanese. The returns of birthplace show that these women mostly come from West Bengal (notably Midnapore, Hooghly and Burdwan), or were born in Calcutta and the neighbouring district of the 24-Parganas. Only 322 are immigrants from Eastern Bengal, or less than the number hailing either from Bihar and Orissa (744) or from the United Provinces (409). Of countries outside India, Japan has the largest share (55) and then Russia (30).

BEGGARS.

114. Similar statistics of the birthplace of beggars (excluding religious mendicants) are given in the last appendix to this Chapter, from which it will be seen that that they number 5,624, that nearly two-fifths were born in Calcutta and the 24-Parganas, and that the majority of the remainder come from Bihar and Orissa and the United Provinces. No less than 2,246, or more than half the total number (4,390) enumerated in Calcutta (excluding the Suburbs), are Musalmans.

OCCUPATIONS BY RELIGION

115. As the Hindus constitute the majority of the population, they naturally predominate in most of the occupations, but there are some notable exceptions. Among those who live by work in jute mills, the Musalmans are nearly as numerous

as the Hindus, the actual proportion being four to five. The former, as might be expected, supply nearly all the butchers, and they form the great majority of the bakers. They further have a far larger share of the workers in building industries than their numbers would warrant, there being two Musalmans to every Hindu. In the printing presses there are five of them to every eight Hindus, and they largely outnumber the Hindus in the tobacco trade. They are also slightly in a majority in the returns for transport: nearly all the Indian lascars working on steamers and ships, and a majority of the boatmen, are followers of the Prophet. The latter also outnumber the Hindus among the cart-owners and carters, the owners and drivers of ticca gharries, coachmen and stable-boys.

One-third of the Musalman population are dependent on industrial occupations, over one-fifth on transport, about one-seventh on trade and one-eighth on domestic service. Less than 6,000 belong to the professional classes, in which they are not only outnumbered by the Hindus (in the proportion of 7 to 1), but are even less numerous than the Christian community. The Hindus divide their energies fairly evenly between industries and commerce, each claiming about one-fifth of their total number. Eleven per cent of them are engaged in domestic service, and 6 per cent. follow the professions and liberal arts. Nearly two-fifths of the Christians find employment in trade, industry and transport, and practically all the remainder man the army, police and public services or follow professional pursuits.

116. There are altogether 624,000 workers, who represent three-fifths of the total population. The proportion of dependants is extremely small, for there are only two to every three workers, which is a very different figure from that returned for Bengal, viz., 7 dependants to every 4 workers. The difference is, of course, due to the fact that so many of the inhabitants of the city are temporary immigrants, who work there only for a time and leave their families at home. The marginal statement shows the proportion for the more important classes of occupations. It may be added that members of the legal profession have more dependants than any other class, presumably because they are mainly well-to-do Bengalis, who have made permanent homes in Calcutta and either can afford large families or have a number of hangers-on.

WORKERS AND DEPENDANTS.

PERCENTAGE OF DEPENDANTS TO WORKERS.

	Calcutta.	Suburbs.
Total	***65***	***83***
Industry	67	89
Transport	39	81
Trade	79	92
Professions	141	141
Domestic service ...	38	44
Unproductive	16	18

117. While 551,125 males, or four-fifths of the male population, are workers, only 72,914 females, or one-fifth of the female population, are actually engaged in any occupation—in other words, there are about 7 male workers to every female worker. The marginal statement shows the occupations which women chiefly follow, and Subsidiary Table III furnishes information regarding individual occupations in which their number is relatively large. There are some occupations which properly fall to a women's lot, such as the domestic industries of rice-pounding and rice-husking and the parching of grain; the proportion of women engaged in such work is therefore naturally large. Midwifery and nursing are also women's work, and it is only to be expected that females should outnumber males in the group (No. 155) which includes midwives and nurses as well as compounders, vaccinators and masseurs. The large number of prostitutes concentrated in Calcutta accounts for their being in a majority in the unproductive class. In no other occupation do women outnumber men, but, considering that in the total population there is only one female to every two males, they are proportionately well represented among fish vendors, religious mendicants, stenographers and typists, and of course also domestic servants.

OCCUPATIONS OF WOMEN.

NUMBERS OF FEMALE WORKERS.

Domestic service ...	22,409
Prostitutes ...	14,271
Industries ...	11,929
Trade ...	8,449

Occupations by race and caste.

118. Statistics of occupations followed by selected races and castes will be found in Table XVI, which is supplemented by the proportional figures contained in Subsidiary Table IV at the end of this Chapter. The latter shows that one-fifth of the Europeans and members of allied races are engaged in trade. Almost as many belong to the army or to the police, while transport accounts for 17 per cent.; the number returned under the latter head includes railway employés, and also ship's officers, sailors, engineers, etc., enumerated on vessels in the Port. Nearly a fifth of the Anglo-Indians come under the category of transport, one-seventh follow professional or artistic pursuit, a tenth belong to the public administration, and a little under a tenth are merchants and their employés: only 8 per cent. are engaged in industrial occupations. Trade in one form or another is followed by two-fifths of the Armenians, *e.g.*, they are actual traders, merchants and contractors or work in mercantile firms; one-fifth are in professional employment, and 9 per cent. have industrial occupations.

The returns for Indian castes show to what a small extent the hereditary caste avocations are followed. Of the Baidyas only a fifth are physicians, and the number of the latter is no more than that of contractors, clerks, cashiers, etc. Only one Brahman in eight is returned as a priest, while one-fifth are domestic servants and one-sixth are traders. Two-fifths of the Kayasths are still writers, and over one-fifth follow industrial or commercial callings. The weaving classes in Calcutta have similarly very little to do with their traditional callings: only 4 per cent. of the Jolahas and 5½ per cent. of the Tantis work as weavers.

SUBSIDIARY TABLE I.—General Distribution by Occupation.

Class, Sub-class and Order.	Calcutta. Number per 10,000 of total population. Persons supported.	Calcutta. Number per 10,000 of total population. Actual workers.	Calcutta. Percentage in each class, sub-class and order. Actual workers.	Calcutta. Percentage in each class, sub-class and order. Dependants.	Calcutta. Percentage of workers to total number of workers.	Calcutta. Percentage of dependants to actual workers.	Suburbs. Number per 10,000 of total population. Persons supported.	Suburbs. Number per 10,000 of total population. Actual workers.	Suburbs. Percentage in each class, sub-class and order. Actual workers.	Suburbs. Percentage in each class, sub-class and order. Dependants.	Suburbs. Percentage of workers to total number of workers.	Suburbs. Percentage of dependants to actual workers.
1	2	3	4	5	6	7	8	9	10	11	12	13
TOTAL ...	*10,000*	*6,064*	*61*	*39*	*100*	*65*	*10,000*	*5,473*	*55*	*45*	*100*	*83*
A.—PRODUCTION OF RAW MATERIALS	*400*	*182*	*46*	*54*	*3*	*119*	*400*	*240*	*60*	*40*	*5*	*67*
I.—Exploitation of the surface of the earth.	*397*	*180*	*45*	*55*	*3*	*120*	*400*	*240*	*60*	*40*	*5*	*67*
1. Pasture and agriculture	381	172	45	55	3	122	332	204	61	39	4	63
2. Fishing and hunting	16	8	52	48	......	91	68	36	52	48	1	91
II.—Extraction of minerals	*3*	*2*	*79*	*21*	......	*27*	...	...	...	...	......	......
3. Mines	1	·45	41	59	......	141	...	...	...	...	......	......
4. Quarries of hard rocks	·02	·01	50	50	......	100	...	...	...	...	......	......
5. Salt, etc.	2	2	98	2	......	2	...	...	...	...	......	......
B.—PREPARATION AND SUPPLY OF MATERIAL SUBSTANCES.	*5,925*	*3,196*	*61*	*39*	*53*	*63*	*6,941*	*3,685*	*53*	*47*	*67*	*88*
III.—Industry	*2,105*	*1,257*	*60*	*40*	*21*	*67*	*4,339*	*2,321*	*53*	*47*	*49*	*89*
6. Textiles	186	132	71	29	2	41	1,663	1,087	65	35	20	53
7. Hides, skins and hard materials from the animal kingdom.	7	5	75	25	......	33	14	10	72	28	....	39
8. Wood	157	104	66	34	2	51	157	83	53	47	1	89
9. Metals	123	67	55	45	1	83	223	97	43	57	2	130
10. Ceramics	13	8	65	35	......	55	104	76	73	27	1	37
11. Chemical products properly so called and analogous.	56	30	52	48	......	91	129	89	69	31	2	44
12. Food industries	105	61	58	42	1	74	187	111	59	41	2	69
13. Industries of dress	538	323	60	40	6	67	1,026	342	33	67	6	200
14. Furniture industries	12	8	66	34	......	51	2	1	41	59	......	147
15. Building industries	307	189	62	38	3	62	516	284	51	49	5	95
16. Construction of means of transport	16	8	51	49	......	95	5	3	63	37	......	58
17. Production and transmision of physical forces	40	27	68	32	......	48	19	13	67	33	......	50
18. Industries of luxury and those pertaining to literature and arts and sciences.	384	193	50	50	3	98	277	103	37	63	2	169
19. Industries concerned with refuse matter.	161	102	63	37	2	58	67	42	63	37	1	58

SUBSIDIARY TABLE I.—General Distribution by Occupation—*continued.*

Class, Sub-class and order.	Calcutta. Number per 10,000 of total population. Persons supported.	Actual workers.	Calcutta. Percentage in each class, sub-class and order. Actual workers.	Dependants.	Calcutta. Percentage of workers to total number of workers.	Calcutta. Percentage of dependants to actual workers.	Suburbs. Number per 10,000 of total population. Persons supported.	Actual workers.	Suburbs. Percentage in each class, sub-class and order. Actual workers.	Dependants.	Suburbs. Percentage of workers to total number of workers.	Suburbs. Percentage of dependants to actual workers.
1	2	3	4	5	6	7	8	9	10	11	12	13
IV.—Transport	*1,331*	*883*	*72*	*28*	*15*	*39*	*1,038*	*601*	*55*	*45*	*11*	*81*
20. Transport by water	554	449	81	19	7	23	197	121	61	39	2	84
21. Transport by road	453	319	70	30	6	42	580	336	58	42	6	72
22. Transport by rail	170	88	52	48	1	94	292	138	47	53	3	113
23. Post-office, telegraph and telephone services	54	27	51	49	...	96	19	6	34	66	...	195
V.—Trade	*1,889*	*1,056*	*56*	*44*	*17*	*79*	*1,464*	*763*	*52*	*48*	*14*	*92*
24. Banks, establishments of credit, exchange and insurance.	82	43	53	47	1	88	44	24	54	46	...	84
25. Brokerage, commission and export ...	150	70	47	53	1	115	40	15	39	61	...	157
26. Trade in textiles	253	138	54	46	2	86	111	45	41	59	1	145
27. Trade in skins, leather and furs	60	38	62	38	1	60	19	11	57	43	...	76
28. Trade in wood	31	18	59	41	...	70	26	11	43	57	...	131
29. Trade in metals	33	18	56	44	...	79	25	14	52	48	...	73
30. Trade in pottery	5	2	40	60	...	149	3	1	49	51	...	105
31. Trade in chemical products	27	17	63	37	...	60	16	8	48	52	...	109
32. Hotels, cafés, restaurants, etc	63	37	58	42	1	72	54	30	56	44	1	79
33. Other trade in food-stuffs	672	399	59	41	7	69	803	438	55	45	8	83
34. Trade in clothing and toilet articles ...	85	59	68	32	1	46	22	11	48	52	...	103
35. Trade in furniture	46	22	47	53	...	112	26	15	57	43	...	75
36. Trade in building materials	7	3	48	52	...	110	8	4	47	53	...	114
37. Trade in means of transport	7	3	44	56	...	128	45	32	71	29	1	41
38. Trade in fuel	46	30	66	34	...	51	49	27	56	44	1	80
39. Trade in articles of luxury and those pertaining to letters and arts and sciences.	124	59	48	52	1	108	73	32	43	57	1	130
40. Trade in refuse matter	1	1	66	34	...	52	1	·54	36	64	...	175
41. Trade of other sorts	197	101	51	49	2	96	100	45	45	55	1	121
C.—PUBLIC ADMINISTRATION AND LIBERAL ARTS.	*1,258*	*550*	*44*	*56*	*9*	*129*	*706*	*287*	*41*	*59*	*5*	*146*
VI.—Public force	*116*	*96*	*82*	*18*	*1*	*22*	*25*	*19*	*78*	*22*	...	*28*
42. Army	54	47	86	14	1	16	4	2	63	37	...	58
43. Navy	...	...	...	...	...	...	...	...	...	...	...	...
44. Police	62	49	78	22	1	83	21	17	81	19	...	24

SUBSIDIARY TABLE I.—GENERAL DISTRIBUTION BY OCCUPATION—*concluded.*

CLASS, SUB-CLASS AND ORDER.	CALCUTTA.						SUBURBS.					
	NUMBER PER 10,000 OF TOTAL POPULATION.		PERCENTAGE IN EACH CLASS, SUB-CLASS AND ORDER.		PERCENTAGE OF WORKERS TO TOTAL NUMBER OF WORKERS.	PERCENTAGE OF DEPENDANTS TO ACTUAL WORKERS.	NUMBER PER 10,000 OF TOTAL POPULATION.		PERCENTAGE IN EACH CLASS, SUB-CLASS AND ORDER.		PERCENTAGE OF WORKERS TO TOTAL NUMBER OF WORKERS.	PERCENTAGE OF DEPENDANTS TO ACTUAL WORKERS.
	Persons supported.	Actual workers.	Actual workers.	Depend-ants.			Persons supported.	Actual workers.	Actual workers.	Depend-ants.		
1	2	3	4	5	6	7	8	9	10	11	12	13
VII.—Public administration (Order 48).	*349*	*146*	*42*	*58*	*2*	*138*	*230*	*88*	*38*	*62*	*2*	*161*
VIII.—Professions and liberal arts	*580*	*240*	*41*	*59*	*4*	*141*	*281*	*117*	*42*	*58*	*2*	*141*
46. Religion	154	81	53	47	1	90	115	61	53	47	1	90
47. Law	115	32	28	72	...	257	38	10	27	73	...	275
48. Medicine	121	43	36	64	1	178	65	22	34	66	1	191
49. Instruction	82	35	42	58	1	136	45	15	33	67	...	207
50. Letters and arts and science	109	49	45	55	1	122	18	9	51	49	...	97
IX.—Persons living on their income (order 51).	*213*	*68*	*32*	*68*	*1*	*213*	*170*	*63*	*37*	*63*	*1*	*170*
D. MISCELLANEOUS	*3,117*	*2,136*	*69*	*31*	*35*	*46*	*1,953*	*1,261*	*65*	*35*	*23*	*55*
X.—Domestic Service (order 52)	*1,229*	*888*	*72*	*28*	*15*	*38*	*531*	*369*	*70*	*30*	*7*	*44*
XI.—Insufficiently described occupations (order 53).	*1,603*	*1,009*	*63*	*37*	*17*	*60*	*1,218*	*718*	*59*	*41*	*13*	*70*
XII.—Unproductive	*285*	*246*	*86*	*14*	*4*	*16*	*214*	*181*	*84*	*61*	*3*	*18*
54. Inmates of jails, asylums and hospitals ...	61	61	100	...	1	...	·06	·06	100	...	...	...
55. Beggars, vagrants and prostitutes ...	234	195	83	17	3	20	214	181	84	16	3	18

SUBSIDIARY TABLE II.—Distribution of the Agricultural, Industrial, Commercial and Professional population in Calcutta and Suburbs.

Occupation.	Population supported.		Proportion of population supported per 1,000 of total population.		Percentage on population supported of—			
					Actual workers.		Dependants.	
	Calcutta.	Suburbs.	Calcutta.	Suburbs.	Calcutta.	Suburbs.	Calcutta.	Suburbs.
1	2	3	4	5	6	7	8	9
Agriculture	31,026	4,496	35	31	42	59	58	41
Industry	188,891	64,624	211	439	60	53	40	47
Commerce	279,595	37,571	312	255	62	53	38	47
Professions	51,940	4,135	58	28	41	42	59	58
Others	344,615	36,314	384	247	64	60	36	40

SUBSIDIARY TABLE III.—Occupations of females by sub-classes and selected orders and groups.

Group No.	Occupation.	Calcutta.			Suburbs.		
		Number of actual workers.		Number of females per 1,000 males.	Number of actual workers.		Number of females per 1,000 males.
		Males.	Females.		Males.	Females.	
1	2	3	4	5	6	7	8
	TOTAL ...	*482,277*	*61,177*	*127*	*68,848*	*11,737*	*170*
	I.—EXPLOITATION OF THE SURFACE OF THE EARTH	*14,543*	*1,578*	*109*	*3,081*	*450*	*146*
	1.—PASTURE AND AGRICULTURE	*13,965*	*1,438*	*103*	*2,702*	*303*	*112*
	(a) *Ordinary cultivation*	9,245	1,316	142	1,568	288	184
1	Income from rent of agricultural land	5,636	1,171	208	337	144	427
	II.—EXTRACTION OF MINERALS	*231*	*1*	*4*	...	...	...
	III.—INDUSTRY	*104,808*	*7,814*	*75*	*30,057*	*4,115*	*137*
	6.—TEXTILES	*10,104*	*1,744*	*173*	*13,609*	*2,311*	*169*
23	Jute spinning, pressing and weaving	9,138	1,615	176	10,817	1,748	162
	8.—WOOD	*8,864*	*444*	*50*	*1,182*	*39*	*34*
36	Sawyers, carpenters, turners and joiners, etc.	8,102	11	1	1,130	6	5
	9.—METALS	*5,897*	*101*	*17*	*1,400*	*29*	*21*
	10.—CERAMICS	*688*	*77*	*112*	*951*	*168*	*176*
	12.—FOOD INDUSTRIES	*4,729*	*704*	*149*	*1,188*	*443*	*373*
56	Rice pounders and huskers and flour-grinders	669	474	709	11	256	23,273
58	Grain-parchers, etc.	117	73	624	108	44	407
	13.—INDUSTRIES OF DRESS AND THE TOILET	*27,596*	*1,304*	*47*	*4,740*	*291*	*61*
68	Tailors, milliners, dress-makers and darners, embroiderers on linen	6,862	258	38	3,006	34	11
69	Shoe, boot and sandal makers	11,427	71	6	531	7	13
71	Washing, cleaning and dyeing	4,080	698	171	780	184	236
-	15.—BUILDING INDUSTRIES	*15,786*	*1,184*	*75*	*3,458*	*430*	*127*
78	Stone and marble workers, masons and bricklayers ...	11,689	1,117	96	1,967	422	215
	18.—INDUSTRIES OF LUXURY AND THOSE PERTAINING TO LITERATURE AND THE ARTS AND SCIENCES	*17,018*	*294*	*17*	*1,476*	*40*	*27*
84	Printers, lithographers, engravers, etc.	6,282	16	2	446	...	...
89	Workers in precious stones and metals, enamellers, imitation jewellery-makers, gilders, etc.	5,994	24	4	763	1	1
93	19.—INDUSTRIES CONCERNED WITH REFUSE MATTER (SWEEPERS, SCAVENGERS, DUST AND SWEEPING CONTRACTORS)	*7,210*	*1,889*	*262*	*435*	*184*	*423*
	IV.—TRANSPORT	*78,581*	*539*	*7*	*8,825*	*28*	*3*
	20.—TRANSPORT BY WATER	*40,084*	*173*	*4*	*1,775*	...	...
94	Harbour works, dockyards and pilots	5,847	155	27	1,115	...	...
95	Ship-owners and their employés, ship-brokers, ship's officers, engineers, mariners and firemen	14,344	...	...	605	...	...
97	*Boat-owners, boatmen and towmen*	9,875	...	...	53	...	...

SUBSIDIARY TABLE III.—Occupations of females by sub-classes and selected orders and groups—*concluded.*

Group No.	Occupation.	Calcutta. Number of actual workers. Males.	Calcutta. Number of actual workers. Females.	Calcutta. Number of females per 1,000 males.	Suburbs. Number of actual workers. Males.	Suburbs. Number of actual workers. Females.	Suburbs. Number of females per 1,000 males.
1	2	3	4	5	6	7	8
	IV.—TRANSPORT—concluded.						
	21.—TRANSPORT BY ROAD ...	*28,316*	*239*	*8*	*4,928*	*27*	*5*
99	Cart-owners and drivers, coachmen, stable boys, tramway mail carriage, etc., managers and employés (including private servants) ...	23,585	206	9	4,394	11	3
103	22.—TRANSPORT BY RAIL (Railway employés of all kinds other than construction coolies) ...	*7,809*	*49*	*6*	*2,029*	*1*	...
	V.—TRADE ...	*88,109*	*6,530*	*74*	*9,318*	*1,919*	*206*
108	26.—TRADE IN TEXTILES ...	*11,957*	*225*	*19*	*648*	*18*	*28*
	32.—HOTELS, CAFES, RESTAURANTS, Etc. ...	*3,159*	*139*	*44*	*435*	*10*	*23*
	33.—OTHER TRADE IN FOOD-STUFFS ...	*31,491*	*4,221*	*134*	*4,932*	*1,516*	*307*
116	Fish-dealers ...	923	561	608	166	236	1,422
117	Grocers and sellers of vegetable oil, salt and other condiments ...	7,797	304	39	1,503	179	119
118	Sellers of milk, butter, ghee, poultry, eggs, etc. ...	3,735	677	181	572	167	292
119	Sellers of sweetmeats, sugar, gur and molasses ...	4,789	183	38	339	16	47
120	Cardamom, betel-leaf, vegetable, fruit and arecanut sellers ...	5,495	1,873	341	664	375	565
121	Grain and pulse dealers ...	5,371	480	89	1,057	320	303
125	34.—TRADE IN CLOTHING AND TOILET ARTICLES ...	*5,201*	*40*	*8*	*130*	*27*	*208*
130	38.—TRADE IN FUEL (DEALERS IN FIREWOOD, CHARCOAL, COAL, COW-DUNG, Etc.) ...	*1,963*	*763*	*380*	*279*	*132*	*485*
	39.—TRADE IN ARTICLES OF LUXURY AND THOSE PERTAINING TO LETTERS AND THE ARTS AND SCIENCES ...	*5,167*	*161*	*31*	*396*	*69*	*174*
	41.—TRADE OF OTHER SORTS ...	*8,691*	*358*	*41*	*695*	*39*	*69*
135	Shop-keepers otherwise unspecified ...	6,418	237	37	396	30	76
	VI.—PUBLIC FORCE ...	*8,568*	...	...	*288*	...	...
	VII.—(ORDER 45) PUBLIC ADMINISTRATION ...	*12,926*	*176*	*14*	*1,257*	*43*	*34*
	VIII.—PROFESSIONS AND LIBERAL ARTS ...	*18,800*	*2,735*	*145*	*1,463*	*255*	*174*
	46.—RELIGION ...	*6,391*	*983*	*156*	*678*	*212*	*313*
149	Religious mendicants, inmates of monasteries, etc. ...	1,261	681	540	326	187	574
	47.—LAW ...	*2,865*	...	...	*151*	...	...
	48.—MEDICINE ...	*3,103*	*803*	*259*	*294*	*33*	*112*
155	Midwives, vaccinators, compounders, nurses, masseurs, etc. ...	670	723	1,079	69	30	435
156	49.—INSTRUCTION [PROFESSORS AND TEACHERS OF ALL KINDS (EXCEPT LAW, MEDICINE, MUSIC, DANCING AND DRAWING) AND CLERKS AND SERVANTS CONNECTED WITH EDUCATION] ...	*2,603*	*497*	*191*	*211*	*5*	*24*
	50.—LETTERS AND ARTS AND SCIENCES ...	*3,908*	*452*	*116*	*129*	*5*	*39*
157	Public scribes, stenographers, etc. ...	269	239	888	...	...	...
161	*IX.—(ORDER 51) PERSONS LIVING PRINCIPALLY ON THEIR INCOME* ...	*3,865*	*2,229*	*577*	*345*	*579*	*1,678*
	X.—(ORDER 52) DOMESTIC SERVICE ...	*58,553*	*21,011*	*359*	*3,937*	*1,398*	*355*
162	Cooks, water-carriers, door-keepers, watchmen and other in-door servants ...	53,019	20,870	394	3,358	1,392	416
	XI.—(ORDER 53) INSUFFICIENTLY DESCRIBED OCCUPATIONS ...	*86,626*	*3,208*	*37*	*9,720*	*843*	*87*
165	Cashiers, accountants, book-keepers, clerks and other employés in unspecified offices, warehouses and shops ...	33,724	290	9	2,185	...	...
167	Labourers and workmen otherwise unspecified ...	48,927	2,873	59	6,525	842	129
	XII.—UNPRODUCTIVE ...	*6,674*	*15,356*	*2,301*	*551*	*2,107*	*3,824*
168	54.—INMATES OF JAILS, ASYLUMS AND HOSPITALS...	*4,089*	*487*	*119*	...	*1*	...
169	55.—BEGGARS, VAGRANTS, PROCURERS, PROSTITUTES, RECEIVERS OF STOLEN GOODS, CATTLE POISONERS ...	*2,585*	*14,869*	*5,752*	*551*	*2,106*	*3,822*

SUBSIDIARY TABLE IV.—OCCUPATIONS OF SELECTED CASTES.

Calcutta excluding Suburbs.

CASTE AND OCCUPATION.	Number per 1,000 workers engaged on each occupation.	Number of female workers per 100 males.
1	2	3
AGARWALA	*1,000*	*3*
Traders	770	2
Industries	17	7
Persons living on their income ...	13	17
Domestic service	63	12
Contractors, clerks, cashiers, etc.	78	...
Labourers (unspecified)	37	2
Others	27	45
ANGLO-INDIAN	*1,000*	*37*
Industries	81	30
Transport	191	5
Trade	95	22
Public administration	101	4
Arts and professions	152	114
Others	380	59
ARMENIAN	*1,000*	*29*
Industries	90	29
Trade	227	11
Arts and professions	201	43
Contractors, clerks, cashiers, etc.	191	16
Others	291	60
BAIDYA	*1,000*	*5*
Physicians	202	1
Income from rent of land ...	87	21
Trade	80	2
Public administration	116	...
Arts and professions	110	.
Contractors, clerks, cashiers, etc.	202	1
Others	203	18
BRAHMAN	*1,000*	*7*
Priests	124	5
Transport	48	...
Trade	171	2
Public administration	56	...
Domestic service	213	10
Contractors, clerks, cashiers, etc.	148	...
Others	241	18
CHASI KAIBARTTA OR MAHISHYA.	*1,000*	*37*
Cultivation	59	10
Industries	188	6
Transport	142	...
Trade	206	17
Domestic service	160	283
Beggars, vagrants, prostitutes, etc.	105	915
Others	140	9
CHINESE	*1,000*	*1*
Industries	780	1
Transport	30	..
Trade	134	1
Domestic service	38	6
Others	25	9
DHOBA	*1,000*	*17*
Washermen	867	17
Industries	38	6
Trade	22	5
Domestic service	18	43
Labourers (unspecified)	20	6
Beggars, prostitutes, vagrants, etc.	9	148
Others	31	6
DOM	*1,000*	*32*
Basket-makers and scavengers ...	644	38
Industries	99	13
Transport	44	4
Trade	25	34
Domestic service	56	90
Labourers (unspecified)	44	21
Others	88	12
EUROPEAN AND ALLIED RACES.	*1,000*	*13*
Industries	68	16
Transport	170	1
Trade	203	7
Public force	192	...
Contractors, clerks, cashiers, etc.	105	11
Others	262	44
GANDHABANIK	*1,000*	*13*
Trade	605	3
Industries	55	3
Domestic service	74	139
Contractors, clerks, cashiers, etc.	90	1
Labourers, (unspecified)	80	3
Beggars, vagrants, prostitutes, etc.	18	1,775
Others	18	23
GOALA OR AHIR	*1,000*	*12*
Herdsmen and milkmen	230	10
Industries	93	2
Transport	156	...
Trade	79	11
Domestic service	21[illegible]	23
Labourers (unspecified)	107	2
Others	121	44
INDIAN CHRISTIAN	*1,000*	*29*
Industries	96	7
Transport	89	1
Trade	60	4
Domestic service	429	31
Contractors, clerks, cashiers, etc.	62	8
Others	264	72
JOLAHA	*1,000*	*9*
Weavers	41	1
Industries	256	17
Transport	130	2
Trade	[illegible]8	11
Domestic service	241	8
Labourers (unspecified)	[illegible]52	4
Others	95	12
KAMAR	*1,000*	*23*
Blacksmiths	250	1
Industries	237	2
Trade	175	13
Domestic service	1[illegible]4	183
Labourers (unspecified)	42	6
Beggars, vagrants, prostitutes, etc.	71	823
Others	10[illegible]	13
KAYASTH	*1,000*	*11*
Writers	45[illegible]	...
Industries	68	2
Trade	162	4
Arts and professions	37	3
Domestic service	87	72
Beggars, vagrants, prostitutes, etc.	48	425
Others	147	12
KHANDAIT	*1,000*	*2*
Landholders	154	1
Industries	206	1
Transport	56	...
Trade	111	1
Domestic service	117	
Labourers (unspecified)	304	..
Others	52	11
KURMI	*1,000*	*7*
Cultivators	97	8
Industries	139	5
Transport	121	1
Trade	141	10
Domestic service	177	15
Labourers (unspecified)	210	2
Others	65	14

SUBSIDIARY TABLE IV.—Occupations of selected castes.

Calcutta (excluding Suburbs)—concluded.

Caste and Occupation.	Number per 1,000 workers engaged on each occupation.	Number of female workers per 100 males.
1	2	3
MAGH	*1,000*	9
Income from rent of agricultural land	489	1
Domestic service	430	2
Others	72	14
NAPIT	*1,000*	*17*
Barbers	470	9
Industries	96	6
Trade	86	11
Domestic service	164	39
Labourers (unspecified)	46	7
Beggars, vagrants, prostitutes, etc.	43	564
Others	96	11
PATHAN	*1,000*	*3*
Industries	172	3
Transport	199	...
Trade	160	3
Public force	73	...
Domestic service	165	5
Others	231	6
RAJPUT	*1,000*	*5*
Military service	143	...
Industries	85	2
Transport	85	
Trade	148	5
Domestic service	270	6
Contractors, clerks, cashiers, etc.	61	...
Others	208	13
SADGOP	*1,000*	*41*
Cultivation	84	69
Industries	136	4
Trade	273	6
Domestic service	194	148
Contractors, clerks, cashiers, etc.	87	15
Beggars, vagrants, prostitutes, etc.	97	6
Others	120	14
SAIYAD	*1,000*	*5*
Industries	201	1
Transport	119	...
Trade	228	2
Domestic service	144	9
Contractors, clerks, cashiers, etc.	64	...
Others	244	12
SUTRADHAR	*1,000*	*13*
Carpenters	410	1
Industries	175	5
Trade	131	19
Domestic service	48	258
Contractors, clerks, cashiers, etc.	104	..
Beggars, vagrants, prostitutes, etc.	39	14
Others	93	12
TANTI AND TATWA	*1,000*	*34*
Weavers	55	1
Industries	182	9
Trade	265	9
Domestic service	157	204
Labourers (unspecified)	101	5
Beggars, vagrants, prostitutes, etc.	93	1,246
Others	147	14
TELI	*1,000*	*14*
Oil-pressers	63	4
Industries	135	5
Transport	54	...
Trade	405	6
Domestic service	80	119
Labourers (unspecified)	99	3
Others	164	39

SUBSIDIARY TABLE V.—Statistics of factory labour.

Calcutta.

Serial No.	Class of Factory, Mill, etc.	Number.	Number of persons employed.		
			Total.	Male.	Female.
1	Aerated water factories	7	362	362	......
2	Arms factories	3	114	113	1
3	Arsenal workshops	1	53	53	......
4	Bakeries	1	33	33	......
5	Bicycle works	2	44	44	......
6	Biscuit factories	1	21	21	......
7	Book-binding works	3	310	310	......
8	Boot and shoe factories	6	445	445	......
9	Brass foundries	12	376	376	......
10	Breweries	1	63	63	......
11	Card-board factories	1	26	26	......
12	Carpentry works	4	399	399	......
13	Chemical works	8	291	288	3
14	Cigarette factories	3	134	116	18
15	Clock and watch works	2	131	128	3
16	Coach-building factories	9	1,325	1,322	3
17	Confectionery factories	4	207	139	68
18	Cotton spinning and weaving mills	1	58	51	7
19	Dairy farms	1	86	84	2
20	Dockyards	1	1,927	1,927	......
21	Flour mills	16	481	449	32
22	Forage presses	4	146	137	9
23	Furniture factories	14	916	905	11
24	Gas and electric light works	4	3,130	3,112	18
25	Glass factories	1	38	38	......

Serial No.	Class of Factory, Mill, etc.	Number.	Number of persons employed. Total.	Males.	Females.
26	Gut factories	1	45	41	..
27	Hosiery factories	1	610	61[illegible]	...
28	Ice factories	3	320	3[illegible]	..
29	Iron and steel works	13	1,657	1,654	3
30	Iron foundries	10	990	988	2
31	Jewellery works	10	743	743	....
32	Jute mills	8	7,896	6,534	1,362
33	Jute presses	5	709	658	51
34	Lac factories	1	36	21	15
35	Leather factories	4	348	348	
36	Lime works and kilns	1	88	88	...
37	Machinery and engineering works	19	3,618	3,613	5
38	Match factories	1	23	23	......
39	Mica works	1	73	41	32
40	Mints	1	922	922	......
41	Motor-car works	7	963	963	.....
42	Municipal workshops	2	392	392	
43	Oil mills	77	2,483	2,173	310
44	Paint works	1	28	28	..
45	Pencil factories	1	24	24	..
46	Perfumery factories	1	27	27	
47	Photo works	4	412	411	1
48	Pottery works	1	89	83	6
49	Printing presses	99	11,880	11,845	35
50	Railway workshops	4	777	777	
51	Rice mills	20	717	[illegible]	-
52	Scientific, optical and musical instrument works	8	822	808	14
53	Soap factories	3	83	[illegible]	...
54	Stationery manufactories	3	104	103	1
55	Stone and marble works	5	295	295	...
56	Sugar factories	8	203	199	4
57	Surki factories	19	542	50[illegible]	41
58	Tailoring works	9	1,090	1,05[illegible]	34
59	Tanneries	7	830	830	...
60	Telegraph workshops	1	847	847	......
61	Thread-glazing and polishing mills	1	35	35	
62	Timber yards	5	180	18[illegible]	...
63	Tin works	1	20	2[illegible]	
64	Tramway workshops	2	622	[illegible]	......
65	Type foundries	4	109	10[illegible]	....
66	Umbrella factories	14	658	65[illegible]	.....
67	Water works	4	147	147	....
	Total	495	53,471	51,054	2,417

Suburbs.

Cossipur-Chitpur.

Serial No.	Class of Factory, Mill, etc.	Number.	Total.	Males.	Females.
1	Arms factories	1	1,644	1,6[illegible]	.....
2	Biscuit factories	1	37	[illegible]7	
3	Bone mills	1	178	12[illegible]	58
4	Cigarette factories	2	554	4[illegible]	1[illegible]4
5	Cotton spinning and weaving mills	1	395	74	321
6	Jute presses	18	5,006	4,9[illegible]1	15
7	Lac factories	1	555	4[illegible]	
8	Lock and safe works	1	87	87	......
9	Machinery and engineering works	1	74	[illegible]4	......
10	Oil mills	7	213	134	79
11	Rope works	11	638	613	25
12	Soap factories	1	35	35	......
13	Sugar factories	1	617	578	39
14	Water works	1	59	59	......
	Total	48	10,099	8,908	1,184

Manicktollah.

Serial No.	Class of Factory, Mill, etc.	Number.	Total.	Males.	Females.
1	Bone mills	2	152	135	17
2	Chemical works	1	167	167	....
3	Dredging works	1	116	115	1
4	Electric light works	1	168	168	......
5	Flour mills	2	48	40	8
6	Iron foundries	1	88	88	......
7	Jute mills	1	1,295	1,05[illegible]	239
8	Jute presses	1	257	207	50
9	Lac factories	1	160	119	41
10	Oil mills	5	277	222	55
11	Silk filatures and factories	1	243	232	11
12	Soap factories	1	48	48	.....
	Total	18	3,010	2,587	422

Garden Reach.

Serial No.	Class of Factory, Mill, etc.	Number.	Total.	Males.	Females.
1	Brick and tile factories	1	121	73	48
2	Cotton spinning and weaving mills	2	2,561	2,403	158
3	Dockyards and Port Commissioners' workshops	2	3,203	3,2[illegible]8	
4	Dyeing factories	1	74	71	...
	Jute mills	2	5,920	4,765	1,155
6	Oil mills	1	59	57	2
7	Rice mills	1	34	8	26
8	Soap factories	1	236	236	...
	Total	11	12,308	10,908	1,400

SUBSIDIARY TABLE VI.—Birthplaces of Beggars and Prostitutes.

Born in	Beggars.					Prostitutes.		
	Enumerated in							
	Calcutta with Suburbs.			Calcutta.	Suburbs.	Calcutta with Suburbs.	Calcutta.	Suburbs.
	Total.	Male.	Female.	Total.	Total.	Total.	Total.	Total.
1	2	3	4	5	6	7	8	9
TOTAL	*5,624*	*3,052*	*2,572*	*4,390*	*1,234*	*14,271*	*12,848*	*1,423*
(A) India	*5,612*	*3,043*	*2,569*	*4,378*	*1,234*	*14,150*	*12,727*	*1,423*
I. Bengal	*3,378*	*1,458*	*1,920*	*2,544*	*834*	*12,807*	*11,526*	*1,281*
BURDWAN DIVISION	*940*	*432*	*508*	*704*	*236*	*5,949*	*5,581*	*368*
Burdwan	162	74	88	143	19	1,191	1,125	66
Birbhum	16	13	3	12	4	55	55	...
Bankura	69	42	27	69	...	369	361	8
Midnapore	291	125	166	220	71	2,265	2,092	173
Hooghly	284	121	163	190	94	1,567	1,517	50
Howrah	118	57	61	70	48	502	431	71
PRESIDENCY DIVISION	*2,292*	*940*	*1,352*	*1,708*	*584*	*6,536*	*5,742*	*794*
24-Parganas	799	326	473	486	313	1,525	1,230	295
Calcutta	1,283	508	775	1,094	189	4,061	3,660	401
Nadia	105	48	57	51	54	491	458	33
Murshidabad	48	21	27	41	7	243	238	5
Jessore	48	29	19	28	20	163	121	42
Khulna	9	8	1	8	1	53	35	18
RAJSHAHI DIVISION	*9*	*7*	*2*	*8*	*1*	*55*	*54*	*1*
Rajshahi	5	5	...	5	...	11	11	
Dinajpur	1	...	1	1	..	2	1	1
Darjeeling	...	...	...	...	...	10	10	
Rangpur	...	...	...	...	...	1	1	..
Pabna	3	2	1	2	1	28	28	...
Malda	..	..	...	...	...	3	3	...
DACCA DIVISION	*119*	*64*	*55*	*106*	*13*	*262*	*144*	*118*
Dacca	59	35	24	55	4	96	72	24
Mymensingh	3	2	1	...	3	81	9	72
Faridpur	32	19	13	27	5	40	34	6
Backergunge	25	9	17	24	1	45	29	16
CHITTAGONG DIVISION	*13*	*13*	*3*	*13*	...	*5*	*5*	
Tippera	6	4	2	6	...	5	5	...
Noakhali	2	1	1	2	...		...	...
Chittagong	10	10	...	10	..	...	...	...
II. (a) Other Parts of India	*2,234*	*1,585*	*649*	*1,834*	*400*	*1,343*	*1,201*	*142*
Assam	13	4	9	13	..	1	1	...
Assam States	1	1	...	1	..	..	...	...
Ajmer-Merwara	3	3	...	3	..	5	5	..
Bihar and Orissa	1,179	827	352	991	188	744	661	83
Baroda	2	2	...	2	..	..	..	
Burma	4	3	1	4	..	6	6	...
Bombay (including Aden)	12	10	2	6	6	12	12	
Bombay States	3	3	...	3	.	1	1	.
Central Provinces and Berar	18	8	8	14	2	18	18	...
Central India Agency	20	18	2	18	2	2	2	...
Hyderabad	4	2	2	4	...	1	1	...
Kashmir	3	3	...	3	...	..	..	...
Madras (including Laccadives)	6	3	3	5	1	8	8	...
North-West Frontier Province (district and administered territories).	4	4	..	4	...	...		...
Punjab	64	51	13	64	...	14	14	
Rajputana Agency	31	23	8	31	...	104	100	4
United Provinces	869	620	240	668	201	409	354	55
French Settlements	...	...	...	...	...	18	18	..
(b) Other Asiatic Countries	*11*	*9*	*2*	*11*	...	*63*	*63*	...
Afghanistan	3	3	...	3	..			
China	2	2	...	2	...	.	..	...
Japan	...	...	...	...	...	55	55	...
Nepal	3	1	2	3	...	7	7	...
Persia	1	1	...	1	...	1	1	...
Turkey in Asia	2	2	...	2	...	...	...	...
(c) Europe	*1*	...	*1*	*1*	...	*53*	*53*	...
United Kingdom	...	...	...	.	...	1	1	...
England and Wales	..	...	...	...	...	1	1	...
Austria-Hungary	..	...	...	...	...	8	8	
Denmark	...	...	...	...	...	2	2	
France	...	...	...	...	...	1	1	
Germany	...	...	...	...	...	2	2	
Greece	...	...	...	...	...	4	4	...
Italy	...	...	...		..	3	3	
Roumania	...	...	...	..	...	2	2	...
Russia	1	...	1	1	...	30	30	...
(d) America	...	...				*1*	*1*	...
America (unspecified)	...	...				1	1	.
(e) Australasia	..	...				*4*	*4*	.
Australia	..	...				4	4	.

B. S. Press—20 1-1913 3436J—656 T. W. L & others.